ACTIVATING
THE ANGELIC

Keys to Releasing the

Holy Spirit and the Miraculous

FLO ELLERS

DESTINY IMAGE₀ PUBLISHERS, INC.

P.O. Box 310, Shippensburg, PA 17257-0310

"Speaking to the Purposes of God for this Generation and for the Generations to Come."

This book and all other Destiny Image, Revival Press, Mercy Place, Fresh Bread, Destiny Image Fiction, and Treasure House books are available at Christian bookstores and distributors worldwide.

For a U.S. bookstore nearest you, call **1-800-722-6774**.
For more information on foreign distributors, call **717-532-3040**.
Reach us on the Internet at **www.destinyimage.com.**

ISBN 10: 0-7684-2706-1
ISBN 13: 978-0-7684-2706-6

For Worldwide Distribution, Printed in the U.S.A.
1 2 3 4 5 6 7 8 9 10 11 / 12 11 10 09 08

DEDICATION

Lovingly dedicated to my precious husband, Mike, who is my childhood sweetheart, my most cherished friend, my comedian in the rough places, and my encourager in the tough times.

In precious memory of my mother, Cleo, and my stepfather, Ray Booth, who—hearing my endless missionary stories—always rejoiced with me and prayed me through to the victory of Christ.

ACKNOWLEDGMENTS

To my Lord and Savior—Jesus Christ, for without Him, I can do nothing. Thank you, Jesus!

To Dr. Gwen Shaw, founder of End Time Handmaidens and Servants, who laid hands on me to write my book. Thank you, Sister Gwen!

In loving memory of my friends: my pastor, George McNeven; my mentor, Art Katz; my intercessors, Mike and Mary Choate; my prayer warrior, Reba Winter; and my eternal friends, Naomi Latham, Mary Ecklund, and Linda Knight.

To my covenant sisters: Rev. Sheila Marks, Rev. Jody Brady, Vicki Lockman, Edna Johns, Georgia Albert, Dr. Margaret Martin, Kathy McIntyre, Ramona Ignell, and Brenda Anderson who always encouraged me and always believed in me. Thank you!

To my apostolic fathers Archbishop Victor Onigbo of Nigeria and Drs. Sam and Kathy Matthews of Oklahoma. And to my special mentors Drs. Rodney and Adonica Howard-Browne and my friends Dr. Jeff and Jane Johns of Indiana, Pastor Mike and Deenie Rose, Pastor Sam and Jennifer Dalin of Alaska, and Pastors Rich and Juanita Massiatt of California.

To Catherine Parmelee, who not only edited part of my book but who has stood by me financially and spiritually all these years. Thank you, Cath, for your faithfulness!

To my trusted friend Rev. Rose Sclafani, who edited my book for content and prayed faithfully for me to finish it. Thank you, Rose!

ENDORSEMENTS

What seminary leaves you without, Flo Ellers' new book will put the finishing touches on in your life. Every person who is serious about ministry, spiritual development, and growth must read this book! While you obtain fresh revelation, this book makes you laugh and cry. With each page holding your attention, it is bound to renew your enthusiasm for real revival in your own life and ministry. If you don't want practical, hands-on, devil-chasing, angelic-appearing excitement; then this book is not for you. If you can't wait to read of the real-life testimonies of a fire brand for God, read on!

Rev. David Woods, PhD
Pastor/International Revivalist

Flo is one who has lost her life for the sake of the gospel. In this process of dying, she has also found many keys to living a supernatural life. In this book, she candidly shares with us her personal challenges, failures, victories, and the keys to living a life marked by signs, wonders, and miracles. You will be inspired and challenged to apply the word of God in your life while developing a deep intimate relationship with our heavenly Father. This book is like "special forces" training for the Body of Christ. This book is a must read for anyone passionate about the army of the Lord.

Tim Taylor
Watchman Ministries International
Renton, Washington

I encourage the reader to peruse this book carefully, allowing it to edify your spirit, as well as to enjoy Flo's insightful teachings. Look at it as a divine treasury in which is stored supplements to nurture your mind, spirit, and soul.

Nita Johnson
World for Jesus Ministries, Inc.
Clovis, California

Signs, wonders, and miracles are set for this new year! So many are looking for their place in God in 2008 and beyond. In this book, *Activating the Angelic,* you will not only find your place in the Body of Christ, but you will also be prepared for that realm in the supernatural called the place of miracles. In all the years I have known Dr. Flo Ellers, I have watched her leadership style in action. She is certainly a warrior in the Kingdom of God, and her stories attest to this fact.

Dr. Negiel Bigpond
Bixby, Oklahoma

Activating the Angelic is an amazing, faith-building, biblical, and factual account of the Old Testament, New Testament, and last century revivals that are still available today if we really want true revival. Flo shares many beautiful, astounding personal experiences of her ministry in the nations where God sent her and worked with her with "signs following!" This book will challenge you to believe God for the same power-packed ministry in your own life and give you the key for how to claim your authority against all demonic powers through the power of the Blood of Jesus as it works through a Spirit-filled person who has paid the price in prophet-length fasts. You will not be the same after reading *Activating the Angelic*.

Dr. Gwen R. Shaw
Founder and President
End-Time Handmaidens, Inc.

The God we serve is a God of plan, purpose, design, and objectivity. Through these processes, He works in seasons— seasons of refreshing, healing, salvation, and manifestations. The word that the Holy Spirit has revealed through Flo in her book, *Activating the Angelic*, is such a fulfillment. These keys to releasing the Holy Spirit and unlocking the miraculous are for these days—God's end-time plans, purposes, designs, and objectives. May all who study through these pages be inspired to rise up and possess a new and precious anointing.

Dr. Morris Cerullo
Worldwide Evangelism, Inc.
San Diego, California

Flo Ellers' book, *Activating the Angelic: Keys to Releasing the Holy Spirit and the Miraculous*, is a fascinating testimony to the present-day relevance of angelic spirits. She draws from a well of encounters in which angels played a very significant role in her deliverance or the deliverance of those to whom she was ministering. I believe this to be a timely book. God is endeavoring to make us aware of both the availability of and the need for angels to help us fulfill our destiny. I believe this book is part of a wave of emphasis on learning to expect and cooperate with God's servants. Angels are sent by the Father to be servants of the heirs of salvation. That's us!

Joe McIntyre, President
The International Fellowship of Ministries
Bothell, Washington

The Prophet Isaiah, in chapter 53, speaking of the Christ who was wounded for our transgressions, cried out, "who shall declare His generation?" The author of this text has answered the cry. In this explosive study of the power of the Holy Ghost, we are captured by His presence even as we begin the first chapter. Dr. Ellers does not only "talk" about this unique person of the Godhead, but she leads you into an experience that will enhance your appreciation of the "Promise of the Father." The experience of the precious Holy Ghost has captivated the heart of Dr. Ellers, and it is evident that she is compelled to bring these truths to us. Isaiah continued, "He was cut off out of the land of the living," but He lives in this vessel and in this manuscript. Novice or veteran of this experience, you will be caught up and propelled into desiring this same type of relationship with the Holy Ghost—You will feel the comfort of the Comforter! The personage of the Holy Ghost will minister personally to you! Herein is the fulfilment of the Psalmist: "One generation shall praise thy works to another, and shall declare thy mighty acts. I will speak of the glorious honour of thy majesty, and of thy wondrous works" (Ps. 145:4-5 KJV).

With great anointing, Dr. Ellers elegantly and aptly declares the glorious majesty of His presence, until there is a sensation deep within our hearts and our spirits cry out for more of the Lord Jesus Christ and His most precious Holy Ghost. May all who read this marvelous literary work echo such worshipful praise!

Dr. B.L. Rice, PhD
President of Shalom Bible College and Seminary
West Des Moines, Idaho

I have been privileged to witness Dr. Flo Ellers impact leaders for the Kingdom of God. She approaches life and ministry with a passion for Jesus, undergirded by a godly character. There is a simplicity and straightforwardness about Flo that is disarming. She comes with the Father's heart and agenda. I commend this book with its practical, biblical counsel. However, I must warn you—this is a dangerous text! It will change you toward a deeper encounter with Jesus and His Kingdom ways!

The Reverend *Dr. John Roddam*
Rector: St. Luke's, Seattle

There is no way any serious-minded believer could discount the value of the contents of this book. In it, Flo Ellers vividly presents the essence of the winds of revival. For anyone who is hungry for a new move of the Holy Spirit, it will spawn memories of past revival eras and challenge hearts to open for the out-pouring that we see on the horizon. I'm grateful to the Holy Spirit for revealing to her Bible principles that open the doors of revival to this generation and perhaps to future generations. This book comes at a time in the history of the Church when the Spirit of God is virtually crying out in every true believer for revival. In this writing, one can literally hear the heart of Flo as she contends for a fresh move of the Holy Spirit in the Church which will produce a Great Awakening in the world around us. May we, the Church, reflect the heart of this book to future generations.

Pastor Bob Rester
Central Park Neighborhood Church
Aberdeen, Washington

I have had the great joy of meeting so many of God's choicest servants. One's life is forever marked by God's true servants. Flo Ellers is one of those true servants of God. I have always been challenged by her commitment and passionate love for Jesus. She has longingly, eagerly, and faithfully sought after God with all her heart. Flo Ellers has been with Jesus and carries that undeniable, authenticating presence that allows Christ to be glorified through her life. This book is a journey walked with Jesus as He has given her keys that have caused her to triumph in and over so many different circumstances. Your life will be impacted by the truth of God's Word, the reality of Jesus' life, and the power of the Holy Spirit as you read this book. The precious Holy Spirit will touch you and change you into the very image of Jesus Christ the Son of the Living God!

Dr. Sam Matthews
Family of Faith Church and
International Christian Leadership Connections Network
Shawnee, Oklahoma

Activating the Angelic by Dr. Flo Ellers is a book that every believer should read. It is not just a great story of her life, but it is also an in-depth teaching on how to walk in the realm of the supernatural. There are many keys throughout this book that will teach the reader how to activate the supernatural.

Dr. Jane Lowder
Director, Calvary Campground
Ashland, Virginia

Flo Ellers has a deep and abiding passion for the lost and for the nations. It is her desire to see others set free just as she has come to know and experience the tremendous delivering power of God in her life. Flo loves the movement of the Holy Spirit and looks to live the Book of Acts, with signs and wonders following those who believe. She has a giving heart and great compassion for the brokenhearted. Her love for the lost leads her to seek revival wherever she goes.

Pastor Jeff Johns
White Horse Christian Center

I believe Flo Ellers has captured God's heart in this book, *Activating the Angelic*. One of the things that Flo talks about is a generation that crosses over. Her emphasis is that we are anointed to preach, heal, and deliver and that there are angels that will not only help us cross over into the next move of God but also assist in bringing the messages necessary for the generations that have yet to praise the Lord. I believe this book will create within you a revolutionary understanding of angels in the last days. This is not just an excellent read, but it is a highly-recommended read for us all.

Chuck D. Pierce
Glory of Zion International Ministries, Inc., President
Global Harvest Ministries, Harvest Watchman

CONTENTS

FOREWORD

Only one who has had direct encounters with the angelic would dare to write a book on the angelic. Knowing the author for more than 25 years, I have no doubt the contents of this book were written by a qualified servant of God.

Flo Ellers has lived a consistent life as a pioneer missionary willing to take daring steps of faith thus placing a demand upon God's supernatural resources, angels. The writer of Hebrews explains that angels are "ministering spirits sent forth to minister for them who shall be heirs of salvation" (Heb. 1:14).

Very few books have been written about angel encounters. It takes a spiritual mind and a sensitive awareness to detect the movements of the angelic in our daily walk. Let me encourage you to read this book with an open spirit: no doubt you will recall times in your own life when angels came to your assistance as you walked through a treacherous situation.

The author clearly explains how God's angels come into play when you are faced with impossible moments. Learning how to activate the angelic can produce a great boldness and an astounding awareness of God's presence in your daily walk. Surely God is releasing more of His mysteries and spiritual secrets in these perilous times to deal with the many satanic, wicked devices unleashed upon the human race (see 2 Tim. 3:1).

I know the contents of this book will leave an impact upon your life, making you more effective in your witness and truly more aware of how God leads and directs your daily walk. Angels are constantly ready to step in and assist. Perhaps they are merely waiting on our call to activate them. With God, all things are possible: "Who maketh His angels spirits, His ministers a flaming fire" (Ps. 104:4).

Gerald G. Derstine, DD
Chairman, Gospel Crusade, Inc., and
Gospel Crusade Ministerial Fellowship
President, Founder, Strawberry Lake Christian Retreat, Inc.
Director, Israel Affairs, International
Bradenton, Florida

INTRODUCTION

Three years after I was born again, I attended the First World Conference on the Holy Spirit in Jerusalem, Israel. It was the beginning of my supernatural walk with the Holy Spirit of God as my teacher and guide. When I returned from the land of the Bible, I shared with anyone who would listen to me all the wonderful truths I had learned from the conference speakers. And then the realization came—for this reason He had apprehended me.

Now set on fire by the Lord, I asked two spiritual leaders to teach me what they knew about the person of the Holy Spirit and His gifts. One told me no; the other did not even respond to me. Undaunted by their lack of enthusiasm, I pressed on, asking questions of ministers who came to our church and devouring any book I could find on the works of Christ.

As I grew in my knowledge of the Word and the work of the Holy Spirit, I told the Lord that whatever He would teach me I would be faithful to teach the next generation. I have kept my promise to Jesus by writing the book you have in your hands. In it, you will find many keys on how to operate in the anointing, how to avoid pitfalls, how to move past your failures, how to stay on fire, and most importantly, how to walk humbly with God and live a holy life.

At the end of your life, when there are no more invitations to minister and you are a faint memory in the minds of those you once ministered to, all you will have left is your walk with the Lord. Maintain *this* relationship above all others.

This generation—your generation—will manifest the power of the Christ in ways no other generation has ever experienced as the Holy Spirit brings the Church back to its pristine glory and the faith once delivered to the first-century disciples. As you demonstrate His glory—give *Him* all the glory.

Chapter 1

THE CROSSOVER GENERATION

Part I: Three Generations

When all that generation had been gathered to their fathers, another generation arose after them who did not know the Lord nor the work which He had done for Israel (Judges 2:10).

It has been my observation that the Holy Spirit moves in three generations of 100-year cycles of revivals, renewals, and times of refreshing. At the beginning of almost every century, the Lord raises up a man or woman who hungers for more of the Lord and uses him or her as His instrument of revival. In seeking and pursuing after Him, these revivalists have an encounter with Jesus Christ, receive a fresh touch of God upon their lives, and then go out to set others on fire with a passion for the lost.

Unfortunately, as the years pass, we can see these turn-of-the-century movements begin to die out. But God is always faithful to every generation, and so once again, another movement begins, and God raises up yet another generation of revivalists. Yet, at mid-century, that second movement also starts to wane in power and purity, so the Holy Spirit again has to train and equip more revivalists until that third generation passes over into a new century—the crossover generation of which you and I are a part. We have crossed over into the 21st century.

We learned about the Azusa Street outpouring in the early 1900s. And we heard about the big tent and healing movement with men like Jack Coe and A.A. Allen in the '50s. The Jesus movement went worldwide a decade later, followed by the Charismatic movement of the '70s, which began in Seattle, Washington, under Father Dennis Bennett of St. Luke's Episcopal Church. This fire of revival spread to the Catholics, Lutherans, Presbyterians, and Anglicans. It was a glorious sight to watch the Holy Spirit jump over the Pentecostal fence (He would not, and will not, be boxed in) into these mainstream denominations. Even Baptists became filled with the Holy Spirit, and they became known as "Bapti-costals." However, as wonderful as that move was, it is now over. But God is about to come on the scene once again in what could become the greatest outpouring since the days of Pentecost.

Today some pray for this move to begin, crying out for a "Second Pentecost." My question is what is wrong with the First Pentecost? When today's generation has attained the fire and glory outlined in the Book of Acts, *then* we can cry out for a second Pentecost. In my view, what the Holy Spirit is about to pour out will be new, fresh, and straight from Heaven. That is not to say that the previous moves were not from Heaven, but it is essential that we are open to the new and not stuck in the past singing, "Throw out the Life Line" or "I Shall Not Be, I Shall Not Be Moved."

If we truly believe we are on the threshold of unprecedented glory, we must press into Him in prayer at every opportunity and seek His face until this move hits America. The richness of this powerful outpouring will cost everything—time, conveniences, and worldly pleasures. But for those who have a heart for God, these restraints are well worth the effort in order to see the Lord's transcendent glory come to earth.

He Is the God of Three Generations

I am the God of Abraham, the God of Isaac, and the God of Jacob... (Matthew 22:32).

"*I am the God of Abraham....*" Everything the Lord gave to Abraham, Abraham received by *faith*. Hebrews 11:8 states, "*By faith Abraham obeyed....*" God uprooted Abraham from his country, separated him from his polytheistic, idolatrous family, and led him to a land of His choosing, promising to make Abraham a great nation. In his unreserved response, Abraham's faith caused him to submit to the dealings of God in the hopes of the glory that would be revealed in the fulfillment of God's promises. No matter how difficult the road, Abraham trusted God and was consistently obedient until he obtained his promise. His obedience brought him great *personal* blessing, and he in turn became a great blessing to others.

Abram's Encounter

When God plans to take you to your next level, you may have a special visitation with Him, like Abram. In Genesis 17:1-22; 18

and 21:1-3, Abram and Sarai had encounters with the mighty Jehovah, and their lives were forever changed. In Genesis 17, Jehovah came to Abram and said that He was changing his name from Abram, which means "a high father," to Abraham, which means, "a father of a multitude of nations." And of Sarai, God said, "*You shall not call her name Sarai, but Sarah shall be her name...and she shall be a mother of nations*" (Gen. 17:15-16). Finally, God said that out of this covenantal union between them, He would give the couple a son—despite the fact that Sarai was then 90 years old! When Abram heard this, he fell on his face and laughed. (I think I would have, too!)

When Jehovah-God made this covenant with this couple, He took the *h* off of His name (which is the fifth letter of the Hebrew alphabet and is pronounced *heh*), and put it on each of their names. In the Talmud, the fifth letter refers to the "breath of His mouth," or the out-breathing of His Spirit. Adding a *heh* at the end of a noun "feminizes" it or allows it to be "fruitful and reproductive." In other words, in this covenantal relationship, Jehovah took the last *heh* from His name and gave it to both Abram and Sarai as part of the covenantal exchange, and they became Abra*h*am and Sara*h*. The *heh-heh*, or the "breath of His mouth," (*Ruauch Hakodesh*—the Hebrew name for the Holy Spirit) caused the couple to become so revived (a personal revival) that they conceived and gave birth to Isaac—whose name means "laughter." I am sure God got the last laugh. Heh, heh, heh; Heh, heh, heh! Come on now, "*Is anything too hard for the Lord*" (Gen. 18:14).[1]

I Am the God of Isaac

"*I am the God of Isaac....*" Everything Isaac received from the Lord, he received by *grace*—he never earned it, and he never worked for it; even his wife, Rebekah, was found for Isaac and brought to him.

Genesis 26 declares that there was a famine in the land at that time. The Lord told Isaac not to retreat to Egypt, because even though there was a famine, the Lord would bless Isaac and his descendants in that very place. God always likes to do things in His supernatural manner so that there is no doubt who is the source of blessing. Verse 12 continues with the story, *"Then Isaac sowed in that land, and reaped in the same year a hundredfold; and the Lord blessed him."* Even though the natural odds were against him, Isaac refused to run to Egypt—which is a type of the world—and God honored his obedience by prospering him *greatly* in that famine-ridden land.

The Passing of the Second Generation

When Isaac and Rebekah were young, Rebekah conceived twins. About the time she was due to give birth to them, they struggled within her. Finally, Esau emerged first with his brother holding onto his heel. Therefore, the second son was named *Jacob*, meaning "heel-holder" or "supplanter."

Years later, when Isaac was old and ready to pass from this earth to his eternal home, he called for his eldest son, Esau, and asked him to go hunting so that he could prepare Isaac's favorite meal. After that, Isaac promised, he would bless Esau before he passed away. Rebekah overheard the conversation and connived with her son, Jacob, to steal the covenanted blessing rightfully belonging to the eldest son. Jacob successfully deceived his father, Isaac, who believed Jacob was Esau. As promised, Isaac pronounced the Jewish father's blessing upon Jacob. When Esau entered the tent, he discovered what had happened, but it was too late for Isaac to retract the blessing. Words are powerful. Isaac (thinking Jacob was Esau) blessed Jacob instead of Esau, who was the eldest son, and Isaac was not able to reverse it. As a result, Esau hated Jacob and sought to take his life. Therefore, Jacob escaped and lived for a number of years far away with his uncle, Laban, eventually marrying his daughters, Leah and Rachel.

I Am the God of Jacob

"*I am the God of Jacob….*" After living a long season with Laban, the Lord spoke to Jacob, and said, "*return to the land of your fathers and to your family, and I will be with you*" (Gen. 31:3). Jacob started home, sending word to his brother, Esau, that he was en route. Then, Jacob heard that Esau was coming to meet him, along with 400 men, and Jacob grew greatly afraid (for he had forgotten God's promise to be with him). So Jacob divided his herds and the people with him into two companies, and then he crossed over the Jordan, while sending a gift to his brother to appease him. You see, Jacob assumed his brother was coming to kill him when, in fact, his brother was probably coming to welcome him.

I learned a long time ago from my friend Pastor Vaughn never to assume anything.

Jacob's Night Season

God allows situations in our lives to change us, even though He can easily prevent certain circumstances by His power or guidance. Nevertheless, He sometimes allows difficult problems so that He can mold us into His character and prepare us to walk with Him for eternity.

The Word states, "*And he* [Jacob] *arose that night…and crossed over the ford of Jabbok…*" (Gen. 32:22). Before change can occur in our lives, we have to cross our Jabbok. Crossing the river at this point is symbolic and is the same as applying the cross to our lives. The cross is where our will and His will cross.

The passage further says, "Then Jacob was left alone; and a Man wrestled with him until the breaking of day" (Gen. 32:24). When God wrestles with a person, His purpose is to test that individual. There is an old adage that says, "Power corrupts, and absolute power corrupts absolutely." Likewise, "pressure reveals, and absolute pressure reveals absolutely." There is a "pressing through" that can only come from the night season.

Moreover, if you will allow the pressures of life to form in you a Christ-like character, you will see the breaking of a new day in your life and ministry.

The story continues: God touched the socket of Jacob's hip, and it went out of joint, but Jacob refused to let go of God. Have you ever had a socket come out of its joint? It causes excruciating pain, but Jacob's tenacity would not allow him to let go until God blessed him. God pressed Jacob for more—it was not enough that he was in the most painful situation of his life—God went on to question him about the most shameful act of his past. *What's your name?* God queried, as only God can. He said, *"Jacob."* With clenched teeth, because of the unbearable pain, Jacob hung on with unrelenting strength while the probing of God drove deeper into his soul. Then, with a relief like the rupture of a boil, Jacob cried out to God, *"Jacob."* He said, "My name is supplanter," which means deceiver.

When at last he finally confessed who he was at the very core of his personality, he surprisingly discovered that God was not angry with him.

31

Instead God made a most remarkable statement to him: "*Your name shall no longer be called Jacob [supplanter], but Israel [contender with God]; for you have contended and have power with God and with men and have prevailed....And [the Angel of God declared] a blessing on [Jacob] there*" (Gen. 32:27-29 AMP).

"*Just as he crossed over Penuel the sun rose on him...[It was a new day for Jacob,] and he limped on his hip*"(Gen. 32:30). God touched the largest muscle—representative of man's strength—and caused that muscle to shrink. As a result, Jacob limped (walked differently) for the rest of his life, no longer relying on his own prowess or shrewdness but leaning instead upon God and His strength.

God Deals With Me

Many years ago, I attended a powerful revival meeting in Kentucky with some friends. At the height of the glory in one particular meeting, the evangelist Rodney Howard-Browne cried out, "Flo Ellers, get down here right now!" As I struggled to get out of my seat (I was already under a heavy anointing), he shouted out again, "Hurry!" So I began to run down the aisle with both arms raised in surrender to the Lord—and when I got within two feet of the evangelist, he reached out and slapped me across the face (at least that's what it felt like), and I was slain by the powerful Holy Spirit. While in that state of ecstasy, I felt a man's hand touching the outside of my hip socket and then firmly applying pressure. I tried to open my eyes and lift my head, but I was stuck to the floor. Almost panicking, I prayed silently asking the Lord what was happening, and said privately to the Lord, "The evangelist said no one is to touch us when we are slain under the power of the Holy Spirit. Who is touching me?" Then I heard clearly in my spirit, "When you get up, go to your [hotel] room and read Genesis 32."

I slowly came out from under the influence of that heavy anointing, opened my eyes, and looked around. To my surprise, no one was left in the meeting except for my three friends who were sitting on the front row, hunched over, looking at me with curious smiles. I asked them, "Where's everyone? What happened to the meeting?" One replied, "The meeting has been over for a long time, and everyone has left!" I smiled weakly and said that I needed to go to my room. My friend reached out a strong arm and helped raise me up from the floor. With weakened knees, I staggered slightly down the hallway to my hotel room. As soon as I entered, I quickly opened my Bible. Not knowing exactly what the Lord wanted me to see in the Word, I turned to Genesis 32 and hurriedly read about the night season when Jacob wrestled with the Lord; *then* I understood the hand on my hip socket and the recent dealings of God in my life. Jesus then spoke to me from His Word, "Flo, I would like all to have tenacity like Jacob of old." He then said some other things to me privately, leaving me with a deep impression that He liked my bulldog faith—a kind that never lets go, that never gives up but continues to *struggle in the night season until the breaking of a new day.* As the years have passed, I have had to rely upon that bulldog faith many times to take me through trials and tribulations into the victory of Christ.

PART II: ELIJAH, ELISHA, AND KING JOASH

In the dark days of idol worship and backsliding in the nation of Israel, God raised up a rough and tough man out of obscurity whose name was Elijah and in whom the Spirit of God dwelled. Elijah came suddenly on the scene and pronounced a judgment of drought to the leaders of his day: *"As the Lord God of Israel lives, before whom I stand, there shall not be dew nor rain these years, except at my word"* (1 Kings 17:1). When the drought ended and the rain eventually fell, a woman called Jezebel (in 1 Kings 19:1-3) re-lentlessly pursued Elijah until he ended up in a cave on a mountain. In the dark of the night, when Elijah was utterly depressed, alone, discouraged, and wanting to die, the Lord came to him and asked, *"What are you doing here Elijah"* (1 Kings 19:9).

Be careful what you pray when you are in such a state of mind, the Lord just might answer your prayer! When the Lord saw that Elijah was not going to change, He told him, "Go, *return on your way to the Wilderness of Damascus; and when you arrive, anoint Hazael as king over Syria. And you shall anoint Jehu...as king over Israel. And Elisha...you shall anoint as prophet in your place"* (1 Kings 19:15-16).

Elijah Finds Elisha

When Elijah found Elisha, he was plowing a field with 12 yoke of oxen. I have ministered many times in Asia and Africa, and I have never seen anyone plow with 12 oxen—maybe two, four, six at the most, but not 12. That vivid picture of Elisha provides an indication of the kind of young man he was. He had great inner fortitude—he had guts. He held great determination to get the job done. He intended to plow that field no matter what the obstacles were!

Remember, in the New Testament, Jesus found His disciples not in a conference frolicking in the river, but fishing, mending their nets, sitting in the tax office—working. Elijah, likewise, found the one he was to mentor to take his place diligently working.

Elijah came up behind Elisha and threw his mantle of power on this next generation leader (but then took it back). Immediately,

Elisha understood the significance of this action, but made excuses, wanting to serve God in his own time. Elisha cried out, *"Please let me kiss my father and my mother, and **then** I will follow you"* (1 Kings 19:20). Elijah responded by telling Elisha to go back to his plow. The sting of that retort must have startled Elisha into reality. Elisha had a change of mind, chose God's best for him, and left the field; he returned the borrowed oxen, slaughtered his own yoke of oxen, built a fire with the plowing implements, and hosted a barbecue for the villagers. His actions made the statement that he determined *never* to look back or return to his past life, but instead, he would serve Jehovah God all his days. Immediately thereafter, Elisha rose up, followed Elijah, and became his servant.

If your calling is that of an evangelist, find an evangelist and serve under that person. If your calling is of a prophet, find a prophet, serve that person, and let him or her mentor you. In that kind of a relationship, you will learn about your ministry in ways you could never learn from a book.

 One powerful lesson you will learn is if you cannot serve, you cannot lead.

Time for the Old Guard to Head Home

About the time Elijah was to go home to be with his heavenly Father, he tested the young prophet three times in order to pinpoint Elisha's heart. The Bible states in Second Kings 2:5 that not only was Elisha aware that his spiritual father was about to depart, but 50 sons of the prophets *also* heard the same Holy Spirit saying that the old prophet was about to leave. After Elisha passed his tests at Bethel and Jericho, it was time for the final test—the crossing of the Jordan River—the place of "death to self." Here the 50 sons of the prophets faced Elijah and Elisha. The sons of the prophets watched, but refused to cross, refused *their* cross. With fire in his eyes, and an uncanny strength in his arms, Elijah removed his mantle, rolled it up, and with great force, struck the Jordan which miraculously divided before them, and the two men crossed over.

I am sure the 50 sons of the prophets forever regretted not crossing over the Jordan. Had they known it was going to be *that easy*, they might have chosen to cross over with Elisha. However, in their refusal to cross "the place of death to self," they missed what the Lord was about to do.

It was not until *after* Elijah and Elisha went on the other side that Elijah looked intently at Elisha and exclaimed,

"Ask! What may I do for you before I am taken away from you?" Elisha said, "Please let a double portion of your spirit be upon me." So he said, "You have asked a hard thing. Nevertheless, if you see me when I am taken from you, it shall be so for you; but if not, it shall not be so" (2 Kings 2:9-11).

The prophet replied that Elisha had asked a hard thing when he asked for a "double portion," because all he could give was *a portion* of what he had received on the mountain. "I can't give you 'double' of what I don't have," he may have been saying. "You will receive a portion of my mantle, but you will have to get your own greater anointing that comes directly from Heaven!"

Godly Distractions

Then it happened. It was *just* another day—nothing special about that particular day—but while they walked and talked *together*, a chariot of fire suddenly appeared with horses of fire (talk about spectacular!), and it swooped in between the men and flashed through the sky. The temptation to turn and look at this flashy sight in the sky—this distraction—was powerful, but Elisha remembered the old prophet's words: *"If you see me when I go, the mantle is yours."* Every muscle in Elisha's body strained to keep his face like a flint and his eyes on his spiritual father as the *Wind of God* swept Elijah off his feet and lifted him into the heavens. Elisha, caught up watching this incredible sight, almost forgot about the mantle. But at the last moment when Elijah was just disappearing from sight, Elisha cried out, *"My father, my father, the chariot of Israel and its horsemen!"* In other words, he said, "My father, my father, I kept my eye on you; I followed you faithfully; I was not distracted; oh please don't forget to drop the mantle!" At that moment, the old prophet disappeared from Elisha's sight, and as Elisha stood gazing into the heavens, the mantle floated gently down to the ground. Elisha looked at it, stepped back, looked again, and taking hold of his own clothes, from top to bottom, he tore them in half, an action representing change, bent over, and picked up the mantle (see 2 Kings 2:11-13).

> For your own protection, change is necessary before you move into a "power anointing."

This part of Elisha's story is similar to that of Samuel the prophet, who grew up in the temple. Around the same time each year, his mother brought him a new coat, and each year he changed from wearing the old, torn, well-used, and out-of-date coat into donning a new, beautiful coat or mantle that perfectly fit (see 1 Sam. 2:18-19).

In my sanctified imagination, I can see Samuel, when he especially liked a particular coat (mantle), refusing to change and looking somewhat ridiculous wearing a coat that was two sizes too small for his current stature, saying, "Oh, but Mommy, I like *this* coat."

"But son, you look ridiculous in it. It's too small." His gangling arms squeezed into a garment much too small for his growing physique. "It is time for a change, son." Hannah said, trying to hide her grin. When Samuel obeyed and put on the new coat—that new anointing—it fit not only the man, but also the purpose of God for which Samuel received that new mantle.

> The Lord knows how to prepare an anointing and fashion a man or woman to meet the current needs of every generation.

Let us return to the story of Elisha. Picture him—after tearing his clothes with fear and trembling—bending over, and in great humility, gingerly picking up Elijah's mantle. I can imagine the moment his hand clutched Elijah's mantle; he must have trembled under the power that was emanating from that holy garment. And perhaps he thought, *What do I do next, Lord?*

> If you are going to "pick up" the power of God, you must do so with humility, always guarding your heart and your thoughts.

I have observed some, who began their ministry in a power anointing, become prideful because of the mantle they carried. As I have watched them, my spirit winced at the display of arrogance. I am fearful of the young prophets and young ministers who strut about in conferences. I never want to see anyone's ministry end in defeat but to see them fulfill their destiny. Elisha walked in humility in a double portion of the anointing, and in humbleness, he served his generation as a prophet of restoration.

Elijah performed eight recorded miracles, and his son-in-the-faith Elisha performed 15 miracles before he died. Elisha cried out for a "double portion," so I said to the Holy Spirit, "Lord, 15 miracles is not a double portion." It was then that He showed me the 16th miracle, which occurred after Elisha was dead and buried. The story is told in Second Kings 13: 20-21.

> *Then Elisha died, and they buried him. And the raiding bands from Moab invaded the land in the spring of the year. So it was, as they were burying a man, that suddenly they spied a band of raiders; and they put the man in the tomb of Elisha; and when the man was let down and touched the bones of Elisha, he revived and stood on his feet.*

On that particular afternoon, when the Holy Spirit had me read for the third time about Elisha's 16th miracle, I asked the Lord, "Why do you keep showing me this story for the third time today?"

 I heard the Holy Spirit say to me with an excitement in His voice, as He gave me the explanation, "Flo! Only a dead man can raise the dead!"

It is time for the third generation to arise!

King Joash

In Second Kings 13:14-19, we find that eventually Elisha became sick unto death. King Joash heard that his father was about to depart, so he visited him. When he saw how sick the prophet was, Joash cried out,

> *"O my father, my father the chariots of Israel and their horsemen." And Elisha said to him, "Take a bow and some arrows." So he took himself a bow and some arrows. Then*

he said to the king of Israel, "Put your hand on the bow." So he put his hand on it, and Elisha put his hands on the king's hands. And he said, "Open the east window"; and he opened it. Then Elisha said "Shoot"; and he shot. [The anointing he was about to receive was for setting the captives free.] And he said, "The arrow of the Lord's deliverance and the arrow of deliverance from Syria; for you must strike the Syrians at Aphek till you have destroyed them." Then he said, "Take the arrows"; so he took them. And he said to the king of Israel, "Strike the ground"; so he struck three times, and stopped.

Don't let an old dying prophet become angry with you! Plunk, plunk, plunk *"…he struck three times and stopped."* With what little strength he had left in his dying body, Elisha likely sat up, looked wide-eyed at the young king, and said to him in a slow, stern voice emphasizing every word, *"You should have struck five or six times; then you would have struck Syria till you had destroyed it! But now you will strike Syria only three times"* (2 Kings 13:19).

> When prophetic instruction is given, fully obey; otherwise, you will miss your "window of opportunity."

When that old prophet laid his hands on the young king—that third generational leader—there was an anointing *imparted* by the laying on of hands.

> You must have more than the anointing; you must also have passion. Plunk, plunk, plunk. Apathy is killing the Church. It was said of Jesus, *"Zeal for Your house has eaten me up"* (John 2:17). It takes more than the anointing; you must also possess strong desire, fervency, and a fiery *passion.*

Several years ago, I ministered in a conference in a large church in Africa, but on that particular Sunday morning, it was the pastor who preached the Word to his people as I sat in the congregation intently listening to him deliver his message with an enthusiasm rarely displayed in most American churches. The pastor preached about Elisha and King Joash. When he came to the part of the story when King Joash was to strike the ground, the pastor had the ushers hand out sticks. He said to us, "Now strike the floor with all your might, and as you strike it, you will be striking out at the enemy, and your children will be saved; their deliverance will come."

Well, just because I am short in stature compared to these precious Africans, I was not going to be left behind, so I took my stick, and just as enthusiastically as the Africans, I struck the ground five, six, seven, eight, ten, fifteen times. The perspiration began to fall off my face onto the floor and then down my back, but I would not give up. We must have struck the ground a hundred times in that sweltering heat, but I was determined to obey to see the fulfillment of the prophet's utterance in my family's lives. We all left the meeting very exhausted, drenched in sweat but satisfied that the Lord had taken note of our passionate obedience.

PART III: SAUL, JONATHAN, AND MEPHIBOSHETH

In days gone by, when the nation of Israel was threatened by the enemy, instead of looking to God Almighty, who was their King and Leader, they went to the old prophet Samuel and demanded to have an earthly king placed over them, just like the nations that surrounded them. (That must have broken Samuel's heart.) Samuel went before the Lord, and the Lord gave the people a king after *their* own heart, a man by the name of Saul, who came from the tribe of Benjamin, who stood head and shoulders over the people. Samuel poured a vial of oil on Saul's head, and indeed the anointing came upon him (see 1 Sam. 8–10). Saul served the Lord for a while, but in the course of time Saul disobeyed the explicit instructions of the Lord and disqualified himself as Israel's anointed king. In the end, the anointing of God lifted off Saul, and he became full of remorse tormented by evil spirits of jealousy, rage, and murder (see 1 Sam. 15).

When those wicked spirits came upon Saul, he called for his armor-bearer, David, to play upon his musical instrument, so the tormenting spirits would depart from Saul. As Saul watched little David play, he recognized the anointing on the young man, the same anointing that *used* to be on him; when Saul would observe *that* anointing on David, he would became enraged with envy and jealousy, and so he sought to kill David (see 1 Sam. 16; 18). In Saul's last days, he became increasingly vile until he was a complete degenerate, seeking a medium—a witch—for guidance, instead of seeking the Lord (see 1 Sam. 28:8).

 Saul started out right at the beginning of his ministry (when he was small in his own eyes), but in the end, he fell into utter defeat, totally defiled and lost his anointing.

The Bible states in Proverbs 19:20, "*Listen to counsel and receive instruction, that you may be wise in your latter days.*" When Paul the apostle was in his latter days, he told his son-in-the-faith Timothy to bring his books, but "*especially the parchments*" (2 Tim. 4:13). A parchment, made from the skin of an animal, was used to write upon at that time. When Paul asked for the parchments, I believe he wanted to write one more book in order to leave a legacy for the next generation.

It seems the enemy of our soul watches us grow in our anointing and calling, patiently waiting until we reach the apex of our ministry. Then he sets out to destroy us, usually tempting us into a sin—a particular sin that brings great reproach to our Lord. Moreover, all the good we accomplished is wiped out in one masterstroke of the enemy's diabolical scheme. In the years that follow, after we depart from earth, the only lasting memory in the hearts of the people is not the good that we had accomplished but that particular sin that brought us down. It is the dead fly in the ointment: *"Dead flies putrefy the perfumer's ointment, and cause it to give off a foul odor; so does a little folly to one respected for wisdom and honor"* (Eccl. 10:1).

So how can we keep from falling into sin in our latter years? Only by forming and keeping covenantal relationships with those who will hold us accountable, pray with us when we are tempted, and help us through difficult situations to keep our ministries intact. Then we can be known in our latter years as people of great integrity—a quality of character desirable in all of God's end-time leaders.

Jonathan Makes a Covenant with David

Saul's son, Jonathan, who was in line to be the next king, also recognized the anointing of God upon David's life. Jonathan realized the kingdom would never belong to him, so he willingly pledged allegiance to David and gave the future king his robe, armor, sword, bow, and belt (see 1 Sam. 18:4). As I see it, Jonathan's character had a flaw or weakness, and it was this: he had a compromising heart. James 1:8 says, *"A double-minded man is unstable in all his ways."* Therefore, Jonathan's heart remained divided between his duty to his father and his covenantal commitment to David, who was soon to reign as king over Israel. At the end of his life, Jonathan left David and went back into battle with his father, Saul, and they both died together on Mt. Gilboa.

When David heard of their deaths, he lamented over them, and he taught Israel the "Song of the Bow," saying, *"How the mighty have fallen in the midst of the battle!...I am distressed for you, my brother Jonathan; you have been very pleasant to me; your love to me was wonderful, surpassing the love of women. How the mighty have fallen, and the weapons of war perished"* (2 Sam. 1: 25-27). What a sad commentary on a life that began with the anointing of God and ended in shame and defeat!

The Third Generation Arises

When the news came that Saul and Jonathan had died, Jonathan's son, who was in the care of a nurse, also heard the news. She became frightened for the child's life, because in those days (and even in some countries today), when a new king rose to power he was apt to seek out people from the previous regime and kill all the remaining family so that they could not become a future threat to his kingdom. This nurse thought David was that kind of a king, so she took Jonathan's son, Mephibosheth, and ran with him to hide him. But while she was running in fear, she dropped the five-year-old boy. As a result, he became lame in both feet.

King David Seeks the Third Generation

In Second Samuel 9:1-13, we find that King David sought out any living relative of his covenant friend, Jonathan so that he might bless them. David sent one of his servants to search. His servant returned and said, *"I have found Jonathan's son who is lame in his feet."*

The king asked, "Where is he?"

"In Lo Debar," the servant said.

Lo Debar means "no pasture"—a place of barely enough. Today there exists a whole generation, like Mephibosheth, who are lame or "walk funny," who have been traumatized, and who live in fear and want. They are in a state of Lo Debar—a place of barely enough. Jonathan's son was brought before King David, and Mephibosheth just *knew* that all of his expectations and the sum of all his fears would be met at the end of David's sword. But instead, he heard the kindness of David's voice as he called him by his name, *"Mephibosheth?"*

He answered with a trembling voice, *"Here is your servant."*

David told him, *"Do not fear for I will surely show you kindness for Jonathan your father's sake, and will restore to you all the land of Saul your grandfather...."* (2 Sam. 9:7), for David was a covenant-making, covenant-keeping man of God.

What? You will show me kindness for my father's sake? Mephibosheth thought. Is this some kind of cruel joke? But he looked into the eyes of David, and he found tears and compassion in the king's gaze. No, this is not a cruel joke. He could see love in the king's eyes. Mephibosheth's defenses began to melt, and he responded with lowered eyes, *"What is your servant, that you should look upon such a dead dog as I?"* (2 Sam. 9:8).

I can only imagine that David thought: *A son of a dog? No! You are the son of a great man! You are the son of my friend Jonathan.* Mephibosheth's heart began to feel strangely warm.

Today's "Mephibosheth" represent a whole generation who hold these same negative thoughts about themselves. Some are "cutters" who cut their bodies to mask the greater pain which lies beneath the fresh cuts and scars of their continual tormenting thoughts. Some are eating out of garbage cans just to get enough food for just one more day. In addition, there are those who were raised in families of neglect, who were never called tenderly by their names, but were screamed at and addressed as "hey you," or "dummy," or were told, "I wish you were never born!" Some of them live under bridges or in stairwells, shielding themselves from the heat and the cold, begging on the street, looking at you with empty, vacant, hopeless eyes.

I imagine Mephibosheth looking suspiciously again into the eyes of King David but only finding love there. Perhaps David smiled and opened his arms wide, and Mephibosheth, surprised at his own response, stumbled over to the king and fell into the arms of his father's beloved friend. There the two wept away the years of pain surrounding the loss of a friend and a father. The father's heart within the king embraced Mephibosheth until all the torment was washed away. *"So Mephibosheth dwelt in Jerusalem, for he ate continually at the king's table and he was lame in both of his feet"* (2 Sam. 9:13).

All Was Restored

All of us, like Mephibosheth, had fallen from grace, and we too did not walk right. Even after we came to know the Lord as our personal Savior, some of us still have a few issues that we are dealing with, and our walk is not perfect. But when we sit at the King's table, eat of His bread (the Word of God), dip it in His oil (His healing power), and drink of His wine (the joy of the Lord, which is our strength) we are being healed of these very issues. Moreover, as long as we keep our feet under His table, no one sees our feet but the King!

Eating at the king's table, Mephibosheth's perspective of who he was started to change dramatically. In the presence of this kind of love—God's love—he would not, he could not ever see himself as a "dog" again. You can only change what you refuse to accept, I heard someone say.

> You can only know what *your* truth is by reading what Jesus says about you.

How can we know the truth so we might be set free? By *"casting down arguments and every high thing that exalts itself against the knowledge of God…"* (2 Cor. 10:5), and by not only believing what the Word of God says about us, but also confessing it out loud for all to hear: *"I am the righteousness of God in Christ Jesus"* (2 Cor. 5:21), *"I am my beloved's and my beloved is mine"* (Song of Sol. 6:3), *"I am the salt of the earth and the light of the world"* (Matt. 5:13-14), *"I have redemption through His blood, the forgiveness of sins, according to the riches of His grace"* (Eph. 1:7), and *"If we confess our sins, He is faithful and just to forgive us our sins, and to cleanse us from all unrighteousness"* (1 John 1:9).

You Must See from God's Perspective

In the decades of the '80s and '90s, we learned who we are *in Christ* (e.g., I am the righteousness of God in Christ Jesus; I am my beloved's). But in this decade, we are learning who *Christ is in us.*

> Without this revelation, we will perish in the battles to come.

I have heard that less than 10 percent of America's youth believe in the Bible! If they don't believe in the Word of God, then they do not have knowledge of what Jesus thinks of them. There is a "Mephibosheth generation" out there, and we must find them.

PART IV: LOIS, EUNICE, AND TIMOTHY

I thank God, whom I serve with a pure conscience, as my forefathers did, as without ceasing I remember you in my prayers night and day, greatly desiring to see you, being mindful of your tears, that I may be filled with joy, when I call to remembrance the genuine faith that is in you, which dwelt first in your grandmother Lois and your mother Eunice, and I am persuaded is in you also (2 Timothy 1:3-5).

As a child, my godly grandmother, who loved me and prayed for me night and day, as she prayed for all in our large family, raised me. I went to sleep hearing her cry out in intercession in her Tlingit Indian tongue *Uk-za-tee* (which means "my Savior"), and I woke up in the morning hearing her praying once again. After I grew up and my grandmother passed away, my mother became a believer in Jesus Christ. Today my mother has taken my grandmother's place and is a great prayer warrior interceding for my sister and me and her grandchildren. I phone her, and we talk almost weekly about the things of the Lord. I cherish those moments with her, because I know that she will soon go to be with Jesus. (My mother went home to Jesus in January 2008.)

There is a principle in the Word of God that states, *"Honor your father and mother...[that] you may live long on the earth"* (Eph. 6:2-3).

The principle is this: Honor brings abundant life.

For instance, Timothy evidently honored his grandmother and mother, for he later proved to be a good leader in the church. He applied the things he learned from his grandmother and mother and from his spiritual father, Paul. Paul recognized Timothy's leadership and encouraged him to pass on what he had learned from him to *"faithful men who will be able to teach others also"* (2 Tim. 2:2). Paul also encouraged Timothy not to be *"ashamed* [to blush or be embarrassed] *of the testimony of our Lord, nor of me His prisoner, but share with me in the sufferings for the gospel according to the power* [dunamis] *of God who has saved us and called us..."* (2 Tim. 1:8-9).

Likewise, we need to encourage this new generation of leaders. We need to *"remind* [them] *to stir up the gift of God which is in* [them] *through the laying on of...hands. For God has not given us a spirit of fear, but of power* [dunamis] *and of love and of a sound mind"* (2 Tim. 1:6-7).

A spirit of timidity should not reside in Christians. You might say, "Well, I was born shy." No, you were not. And even if you were, you are now born-again, and you have now been given a spirit of *dunamis* and of love and of a calm, well-balanced, and disciplined mind. You have self-control, because the power of the Holy Spirit lives in you. You just have to learn how to yield yourself (spirit, soul, and body) to Him. You have the spirit of dominion in you, because Jesus lives in you. You just have to stir up that gift, rekindle the embers. How? Jude 1:20 states, *"But you beloved, building yourself up on your most holy faith, praying in the Holy Spirit."* The Amplified Bible says we will rise higher and higher as an "edifice." An *edifice* is a "fine building." An examination of the Greek text reveals that this means He is progressively forming something in us as we pray with the Holy Spirit. As we pray in our spiritual language, we are moved in our spirits to accomplish all of God's ultimate plan for our lives and ministries.

If you are not baptized in the Holy Spirit, then you can be right now. Do you want to be filled right now? Then please get on your knees and pray with me:

Father, I am a believer in Your Son Jesus Christ. I believe He died for me, and I believe He was raised for me from the dead by the power of the Holy Spirit. I have confessed I was a sinner, and I asked Him to be my Savior and to be Lord over my life. I have read in the Book of Acts that the disciples in the upper room were filled with the Holy Spirit and began to glorify You in a heavenly language they had never learned before. I desire to be filled with Your Spirit in the same way and to speak in a new language so I can praise You and rekindle my passion for You. So Jesus, I ask You to baptize me in the Holy Spirit right now. I thank you that I can trust You when I ask for the baptism of the Holy Spirit; I will not receive any other spirit but Your Spirit and power. In faith right now, I will open my mouth to praise You, but I will not say one word in English or any other word from any language I may know. I ask You to fill me right now Jesus with the same power that You filled the disciples with in the upper room. I receive now.

All right, just lift your hands now and start to praise Him. Now stop. Now start praising Him in your heavenly language again. Now stop. You can start and stop at will. Pray every day for a minimum of 15 minutes in your new language until you are enveloped in His presence. As He continually fills you, you will begin to grow in His love and operate in His gifts, and there will be a stirring passion within you for the lost. When you leave His presence, His love and anointing will flow out of you to everyone you met.

We are the Crossover Generation

We are that *third* generation that just crossed over from the 20th century into the 21st century. As in the very beginning of previous centuries, prepared groups of new leaders are ready for the new move of God that stands at the very door of the Church.

If you are not ready, you can get ready:

Just like Jacob of old, you will have to *struggle in the night season until the breaking of your new day.*

Like King Joash, you will need more than the anointing imparted to you, you will need *great and ardent passion.*

Like Mephibosheth, you will need to *renew your mind* until you bring every thought captive to the obedience of the Christ, seeing yourself as Jesus sees you.

In addition, like Timothy, you can *pray with the Holy Spirit in your heavenly language* until the gift within you is so stirred it is like glowing embers that have burst into passion for Jesus—becoming a mighty flame of revival for your generation.

ENDNOTE

1. For more information, go to http://www.hebrew4 christians.com.

Chapter 2

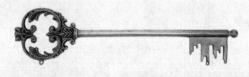

ANOINTED TO PREACH,
HEAL, AND DELIVER

Jesus said to His disciples, "*Behold, I send the Promise of My Father upon you; but tarry in the city of Jerusalem until you are endued with power from on high*" (Luke 24:49).

The commandment given to the Church to "*tarry...until...*" has never been rescinded or taken back. When the Holy Spirit came on the Day of Pentecost, He came with power. It is true the 120 disciples spoke in tongues in the upper room in Acts 2, but what they received was power.

Let me explain it with this illustration. I have a particular pair of sharp-looking shoes that I like to wear. They look like the kind my grandfather wore when I was a child. They have four holes that lace up to hold the "tongue" in place. When I went to the specialty shoe store, I did not say to the salesperson, when she asked what I wanted, "I want a pair of *tongues*." If I would have said that, she would have rolled her eyes back and thought, "This lady's elevator does not go to the top!" That is a rather humorous illustration, but that is what most Pentecostals and Charismatics think: they think they have received "tongues" when baptized in the Holy Spirit.

 No, you *speak* in tongues, but what you received is *power* from on high. You got the pair of shoes (the power), and the tongues just came along with them to help release the power.

The early Pentecostals knew what it was to *tarry* in His presence *until* they were *endued* or clothed with *power from on high*. A great minister once said, "If I am a man of God, endued with power from On High, souls will break down under my preaching; if I am not, nothing out of the ordinary will take place. Let this be the test for every preacher. By this, we stand or fall."[1]

The old-time Pentecostals used to walk in great power. When I was very young, I remember vividly watching this precious Pentecostal woman worship the Lord. When she began to weep in the presence of the Lord, she would take her white hankie out, wipe her tears, and then re-tuck it back under the cuff of her blouse or dress. She was a plain-looking woman and wore her hair in what we called the "Pentecostal bun," but I tell you, if it would take putting my hair up in a bun to have the kind of power she had with the Lord, I would gladly wear my hair like that. However, thank God, He has delivered us from "bun-dage."

 It is not in our holiness that we move in power, but power comes from an intimate relationship with Jesus.

When the Holy Spirit used Peter to heal the lame man in Acts 3, the people marveled at Peter as if he had done that glorious miracle. Peter, walking in great humility, said to the crowd, "*Ye men of Israel, why marvel ye at this? Or why look ye so earnestly on us, as though by our own power or holiness we made this man to walk*" (Acts 3:12 KJV).

THOSE WHO WAIT

He gives power to the weak, and to those who have no might He increases strength. Even the youths shall faint and be weary, and the young men shall utterly fall, but those who wait on the Lord shall renew their strength... (Isaiah 40:29-31).

The promise is there: "*those who* **wait** *on the Lord shall renew their strength.*"

 Basking in His presence in prayer, praise, worship, reading of the Word, praying in your heavenly language, and then sitting in silence will cause you to rise above any negative circumstances you may be going through.

Soaking in His presence will cause you to make progress in your spiritual walk like nothing else can. *It* will change you. It will make you bold and kind. It was said of Peter and John, in Acts 4:13, "*Now when they saw the boldness of Peter and John, and perceived that they were unlearned and ignorant men, they marveled; and they took knowledge of them, that they had been with Jesus*" (KJV).

Isaiah the prophet said those who "wait" on the Lord would become strong in the spirit. The word *wait* in *Strong's Concordance* means "to bind together; perhaps by twisting; fig – (1.) to expect; (2.) to look; (3.) to tarry."[2] Ecclesiastes 4:12 says, *"Though one may be overpowered by another, two can withstand him. And a threefold cord is not quickly broken."* While waiting in His presence, you become bound together, entwined—The Lord, Holy Spirit, and you—and when the trials of life come to try you (and they will), you will not be broken, confused, or greatly shaken.

"EXPECTING TO RECEIVE…"

Expectation maintains our hope and makes us steadfast. Again in Acts 3, when Peter and John went to the temple to pray, they came across an invalid who was sitting by the temple gate asking for money from those on their way to church. When Peter realized that he did not have any money to give, he said to the crippled man, *"'Look at us!' So the man gave them his attention, expecting to receive something from them"* (Acts 3:4-5).

Expectation is your key to your miracle!

This poor, invalid man looked for money for his next meal from anyone who would have compassion on him, but what he received that day was so much more than what he expected. He cried out to the passersby, "Alms, alms, alms." And he got, "legs, legs, legs!" (Alms were acts of charity solicited by the unfortunate.) Peter did not have any money, but he was rich in faith and in the power of God. This power comes from a relationship with Jesus. That is where Peter and John were going when they encountered the invalid man; they were going back to the temple to pray to Jesus to maintain this intimacy with Him. It is the same with us: while we stay in that place of intimacy with the Lord and cry out to Him, He will take note of the intensity of our heart's cry and answer us. When the world cries out to us, we will have something to give to them, *"Such as I have give I thee…"* (Acts 3:6). Our *looking*, our *tarrying*, our *waiting*, and our *expectation* will bring great reward.

In our times of prayer, He exchanges our weakness for His strength, our inability for His ability, and our faintheartedness for His boldness. Moreover, our impossibilities will become possible when we come out of our prayer closet: *"Such as I have give I thee…."*

JESUS OUR PATTERN SON

In the Genesis account, man was made in the *image of God*. However, because of man's sin, satan defeated man in the Garden of Eden. In the New Testament, God came to earth in the *image of man—Jesus—*to defeat satan and undo what he had done to His precious creation. Jesus was fully God and fully man. Unlike the first man Adam, Jesus became the "last Adam" (see 1 Cor. 15:45), and defeated satan first in the wilderness, then in the garden, and ultimately on the Cross.

As we look at the Son of God, Jesus, we can examine His life and see how God the Father anointed Him to defeat satan, and then we can apply those principles to our lives so we can walk in the same anointing that Jesus walked in on this earth.

GOD THE FATHER PREPARES A BODY

When Jesus left His heavenly abode, He also left behind all the glories of Heaven and came to earth as a babe. In Hebrews

10:5, it says, *"Therefore, when He came into the world, He said: 'Sacrifice and offering You did not desire, but a body You have prepared for Me.'"*

Just as God the Father prepared a body for His Son to work through while He was on earth, so now the Son is preparing a Body for the Holy Spirit to flow through with His gifts. The leaders in this Body are the gifts given to the Church from Jesus, listed in Ephesians—apostle, prophet, evangelist, and pastor/teacher—and they are given *"for the equipping of the saints for the work of the ministry, for the edifying of the **body** of Christ…"* (Ephesians 4:12-13). *Christ*, according to *Strong's Concordance*, means "anointed."[3] That same anointing that the Father poured upon Jesus—the Head of the Body—will also flow down over His Body (us) to do the same miraculous works that Jesus did.

> The secret to releasing that anointing is to learn how to yield not only your spirit and soul to Him but also your body.

JESUS' EARLY YEARS

Just as our body, soul (or mind), and spirit must mature and develop, Jesus' body, mind, and spirit needed to develop. Luke 2:40 states, *"And the Child [Jesus] grew and became strong in spirit, filled with wisdom; and the grace of God was upon Him."* As a Hebrew child, Jesus spent countless hours studying and memorizing the Torah (the Pentateuch), which is the first five books of the Bible—Genesis, Exodus, Leviticus, Numbers, and Deuteronomy: *"and the grace of God was upon Him."* *Strong's Concordance* indicates that *grace* means the "graciousness, of manner or act; especially the divine influence upon the heart and its reflection on the life, including gratitude; acceptable, benefit, favor, gift, grace, gracious, joy, liberality, pleasure, and thankworthy."[4] The *grace* of God is not only divine favor, but it is *also* the divine gift of God upon a life. The Bible says Jesus was *"full of grace and truth"* (John 1:14b).

 That was His anointing—to be full of grace and truth (the Word). Being full of the Word was Jesus' *first* anointing.

Jesus' Submission

When Jesus was only 12 years old, instead of going home with His parents after they had all observed the Feast of the Passover, He stayed behind in Jerusalem because He wanted to be in His Father's House (the temple). At that tender age, He already knew in His heart and mind who He was, and He felt He *must* be doing His Father's will. When His earthly parents, Joseph and Mary, discovered that He was missing from the caravan, they returned to Jerusalem and found Him in the temple sitting in the midst of the teachers of the Law. They were all amazed at His spiritual knowledge as they watched this young child who was not only listening to the scholars but also asking them pointed questions. Mary then took Jesus aside and chided Him for not letting them know His whereabouts. Jesus was baffled; why did His mother not understand the reason He must be in Father's House? After all, she had known from His birth of His divinity and destiny, but Mary had forgotten the moments that she pondered her Son's calling and reacted as any good Jewish mother would. After that incident in the temple, the Bible makes a startling statement about Jesus; it says, in Luke 2:51-52, *"Then He went down with them* [his parents]...*and was subject to them…*[and the result was that] *Jesus increased in wisdom and stature, and in favor with God and man."*

Submission to authority was Jesus' key to increase. He increased or grew mentally (*in wisdom*), physically (*in stature*), spiritually (*in favor with God*), and socially (*in favor with man*). He was well balanced in all four areas of His life. If Jesus is the pattern of our lives, we must strive to maintain this same balance.

Each area of our lives (spiritual, mental, physical, and social) will jostle for supremacy, but as we contend to keep Jesus and the things of the spirit central in our lives, we too will increase and walk a balanced life.

JESUS BEGINS HIS MINISTRY

As the people listened to a firebrand of a preacher—John the Baptist—they sat in awe of this radical minister and wondered if he might be their promised Messiah. John must have sensed their longing hearts, because he said to them, *"I indeed baptize you with water unto repentance, but He who is coming after me is mightier than I, whose sandals I am not worthy to carry. He will baptize you with the Holy Spirit and fire"* (Matt. 3:11). On one particularly beautiful morning, after most of the people had been baptized in the cool River Jordan, John saw his cousin Jesus coming toward him. As he squinted to block out the early morning sun, he did a double take: suddenly John did not just see his cousin coming toward him, for the Holy Spirit must have spoken to him: "John, this is not your cousin, this is your Messiah!"

As the revelation of who Jesus was flooded John's mind, John opened wide his mouth and thundered in a booming voice for all to hear, *"Behold! The Lamb of God who takes away the sin of the world"* (John 1:29). The stunned crowd slowly turned in unison to look upon their Messiah in silent recognition as they stood in awe, giving reverence to their God who had come to take away the sin of the world. Did you notice John did not say *"who takes away the sins of the world"* (plural)? He said, *"who takes away the sin of the world."* What was the "sin" he referred to? It was *the sin of rebellion* toward God—the attitude of "I'll do it my way." When Eve was about to yield to satan's temptation of rebellion toward God in the Garden of Eden, the serpent said to her, *"For God knows that in the day you eat of it your eyes will be opened, and you will be like God, knowing good and evil"* (Gen. 3:5). The ultimate (new age) lie of satan has never changed, and it is this: you shall be like God without God!

When Jesus came close to John to be baptized by him, John tried to prevent Him, saying, *"I need to be baptized by You, and are You are coming to me?"* In other words, John said, "I am the sinner and You are the Messiah, the Savior!" Jesus replied, "No John, do it to fulfill the Word; do it John, for I need to be an example" (my paraphrase, see Matt. 3:13-15).

The River Jordan, the place of Jesus' baptism, is in typology, the "place of death." It flowed into the Dead Sea, where sins were washed away and the people entered into newness of life. When Jesus went down into that "place of death," He did not go to have His sins washed away, for He was sinless, but He went into that watery grave to die to His own will. It was a symbolic gesture. From that point on, He was no longer Mary's boy or Joseph's son, but had *now* entered into His destiny as the promised Messiah—the Savior of the world.

ONE OBEDIENT ACT OPENS HEAVEN

Luke's account further describes the river scene of Jesus at the Jordan, *"...while He prayed, the heaven was opened"* (Luke 3:21). (It was also by a river that Ezekiel saw the glory of God, that Daniel saw the vision of the last days, and that John had his revelations of the water of life.) I wonder what Jesus prayed by that river? Whatever He prayed so impressed the Father that it caused Him to hear and open the heavens. The Father responded to His Son by sending the Holy Spirit to earth. This was Jesus' *second* anointing: *"in bodily form like a dove,"* the Holy Spirit descended upon Jesus, *"and a voice came from heaven which said, 'You are my beloved Son; in You I am well pleased"* (Luke 3:22).

One prayer, one act of obedience opened the heavens, and the Holy Spirit came upon Jesus in power, and the Bible says, He *remained* upon Him (see John 1:32). The Father expressed His pleasure with His Son—even though, up to that time, Jesus had yet to perform one miracle, had yet to finish a 40-day fast, and had yet to pray all night on a mountain. That is to say, the Father loved Jesus, not for His deeds or works but simply because He was His Son. The Bible says in First John 3:2, *"Beloved, now are we the sons of God..."* (KJV). We are sons and daughters of God, and just as God the Father loved His Son, He loves us!

JESUS TEMPTED

After that river encounter, Jesus was *"filled with the Holy Spirit"* (Luke 4:1), and the glory of God came upon Him. However, as great as that glory was, Jesus did not go into full-time ministry or book an international evangelistic crusade, but instead, He further submitted to His Father's wisdom as the Holy Spirit *"led Him into the wilderness"* (Luke 4:1). The wilderness is a place of extremes—high heat during the day and frigid cold during the night. For 40 days, Jesus was tried and tested, and the Word says, *"He ate nothing, and afterward, when they had ended He was hungry"* (Luke 4:3).

I have been on several lengthy fasts—two lasting 40 days—and at the end of those fasts, I did not experience hunger. I do not believe Jesus was merely hungry for food; rather, He was hungry for a move of God. He was hungry to see the blind eyes open, the lame walk, the deaf hear, the dumb talk, the lepers cleansed, and the dead raised back to life!

> If you find yourself in a wilderness experience, do not curse your wilderness, for it is your place of preparation for your ministry. It is a place where you will have a face-to-face encounter with yourself and see yourself the way you really are! You may not like what you see, but it is worth finding out.

THE TEMPTATIONS

The Lord's temptations in the wilderness were very real temptations that tested every fiber of His resolve to press through to victory—not only for Himself, but also for us, for humanity. The first temptation was against His fleshly appetites, but Jesus vehemently resisted. The second temptation was powerful, but Jesus held steady and withstood satan's advances. In that temptation, Jesus did not debate with satan about the authority delivered to Him but held steady. In the third temptation, when satan tried to get Jesus to prostrate before him in worship, Jesus refused to give the *"god of this age"* any worship (see 2 Cor. 4:4). In that last temptation, satan tried to get Jesus to display Himself in a showy way; again Jesus resisted the temptation to settle the issue: "If you are the Son of God...."

Jesus knew full well who He was. He had known since He was 12 years old. He knew why He came to earth. Moreover, He knew that He was the Messiah—the Son of God—but He would not submit to the lust of the moment to prove His divinity, nor would He bow to take back the authority that satan boasted of having. God the Father had a plan to take back all that Adam and Eve had lost, but He would do it through His Son, in His own time, and in His own way.

The Bible clearly states that there are three areas of temptations: "*the lust of the flesh, the lust of the eyes, and the pride of life...*" (1 John 2:16). Eve, tempted by satan in all three areas, succumbed to all of them. She saw the "*tree was good for food*" (which is the lust of the flesh), "*pleasant to the eyes*" (the lust of the eyes), and "*a tree desirable to make one wise*" (the pride of life). (See Genesis 3:6.)

When Jesus was in the wilderness, He was also tempted in these identical areas. He was tempted in the flesh, "*If you are the Son of God, command that these stones become bread*" (Matt. 4:3). He answered with what He had learned and memorized as a child from the Book of Deuteronomy: "*It is written, 'Man shall not live by bread alone, but by every word that proceeds from the mouth of God'*" (Matt. 4:4). When He was tempted with the lust of the eyes (the devil showed Him all the kingdoms of the world in a moment of time), He refused to submit to any will except His Father's in order to "win back" the authority and the glory man had lost in the Garden. Again, Jesus resisted the enemy with the Word: "*For it is written...*" Again, the challenge came to Him, "*If you are the Son of God...*" Jesus refused the taunting of the devil and would not give in to the sin of the "pride of life." When the devil was not able to cause Jesus to sin, the Bible says that satan left Him for an *"opportune time"* (Luke 4:13).

The devil has many years of experience in the art of temptation, and he has won many victories; he has great patience to wait for another moment of weakness to tempt a man or woman.

> He tempts us in areas of weakness, but he also tempts us in areas of strength, which is the most subtle move of all; for in the place of strength, you presuppose you cannot fall, which is the sin of pride.

The next opportunity satan took advantage of Jesus' humanity was when He was interceding for us in the Garden of Gethsemane—the place of the "wine press" where Jesus submitted to His Father's will to drink the cup of suffering for us. For three hours of agony, Jesus prayed more earnestly that God's desire and plan be done in His life: *"Father, if it is Your will, take this cup away from Me; nevertheless not My will, but Yours, be done"* (Luke 22:42).

The last temptation of Christ came when He was on the cross. (See Matthew 27:41-44.) It was the place of His final surrender and the place of His greatest extremity; there, He was most vulnerable to the last three tauntings of satan as the people wagged their tongues at Him and mocked, *"He saved others; Himself He cannot save. If He is the King of Israel, let Him now come down from the cross, and we will believe Him. He trusted in God; let Him deliver Him now if He will have Him; for He said, 'I am the Son of God'"* (Matt. 27:41-44).

No other battle that Jesus encountered with satan could eclipse that moment! Because He did not yield to the three temptations in the wilderness, and because He won the victory in the

Garden of Gethsemane, the final three temptations had no sway over Him. As every limb slowly pulled out of joint, and the pain of every sin of humanity was upon Him, Jesus cried out a second time and yielded up His spirit. What appeared to satan and to his demons as a victory turned out to be satan's worst nightmare! The battle was won for all ages to come—Jesus, the Victor!

The devil tries to destroy you at the beginning of your ministry, but he particularly tries at the end. If you do not pass *your* tests, *your* temptations in the "wilderness," *your* "wine press," he will come at you in your most vulnerable time and his most opportune moment to bring you to shame and to disgrace Christ. The Word says in Job 8:7, "*Though your beginning was small, yet your latter end would increase abundantly.*"

Fight the battle of the "*lust of the eyes, the lust of the flesh and the pride of life*" before you start your ministry; and in your end, like Paul the apostle at the end of his life, you too will ask especially for "*the parchments*" (see 2 Tim. 4:13) so you can write your final chapter and leave a legacy for the last generation.

MY 40-DAY FAST

Years ago, I traveled with a small team of seasoned ministers to the Philippines where we held a minister's conference on Mindanao Island. At the end of our trip, we went to a church to preach the Word, believing for signs, wonders, and miracles to follow. Just before the service started, the pastor asked us if we would come to his office and help deliver a woman who was demon possessed. We quickly agreed (*of course* we will come and help—we are from America). We went back to his office, but we soon found that we were ill-equipped for the kind of spiritual battle that followed. We were in over our heads! Once we identified the possessed woman in the room full of onlookers, we pounced on her like warriors itching for a fight. With all of the authority we could muster, we commanded the evil spirit to "Come OUT in Jesus' NAME!" All of a sudden, I began to sense *something* was coming up out of this woman, so I said, "Here it comes, here it comes…" No sooner had the words come out of my mouth, than she opened her pursed lips and looked as if she was going to spit *something* out. To my amazement she spit out something resembling a watermelon seed! Undeterred, we pressed on: "I said, come OUT in the Name of JESUS!" Again, I perceived in my body that *something* was coming out of her; this time I simply thought, "*Here it comes….*" But to my chagrin, she spit out another seed or pit of some kind, all the time, looking at us with a mocking jeer. When she did *that*, I found myself doubling up my fist, and I went instantly from moving in the Spirit to wanting to do something in the flesh that I would regret. When that demon in her mocked me, I attacked her *and* that spirit, but of course, nothing happened.

> Nothing done in the flesh will produce the desired spiritual results.

When the leader of our group saw my flesh rising, he said, "Flo, the people are waiting out in the church for the Word, so you go out there and preach, and we will handle the deliverance." With that instruction, I left the room, went back into the church, and sat down on the front row, seething inside, while a steady stream of perspiration flowed down the middle of my back, staining my beautiful dress.

When the enthusiastic praise was over, the pastor went to the platform and introduced me. I stood erect, walked up to the platform with great determination, and still somewhat miffed at the mocking of that demon, I said with a forceful opening, "Open your Bibles to..." I do not recall what I preached, but by the time I was coming to the end of my fiery message, I was spitting mad at the devil! (In addition, some of those "white cotton balls" were falling on the people as I marched back and forth, too close to the front row.) At the conclusion of my message, I told the audience what had happened in the back room and that I was going home to begin a 40-day fast in order to gain the spiritual authority and anointing to cast out devils. Therefore, I left the island of Mindanao with decisiveness in my spirit to win.

After returning home and resting sufficiently from my Asian trip, I talked with my husband about my commitment to shut myself away with the Lord. I asked him if he would be in agreement with me about going on a 40-day fast. I then read to him what the Bible says about abstaining from marital intimacy while on the fast (see 1 Cor. 7:5). I asked him again, and he just stared at me as if thinking deeply about it. At that time, I was a bit heavier than I am now, and so he looked at me for a long moment; then his eyes quickly looked me over from head to foot (I am sure he was thinking about all the weight I would lose!), and he spouted out with a grin, "Go for it!" With that permission, I went for it.

Months following that fast, I was invited to another Asian country to do some revival meetings. After arriving at the airport, I was taken to a home where I quickly unpacked, slept, and with great excitement in my spirit, went to my first meeting. There I preached on the power of God and gave my first altar call. Many responded; so after the ushers got the people lined up, I began to go down the ministry line. I laid my hands on the first person, and down she went, then the next one, and then the third—down they went, slain by the power of God.

By the time I was halfway down the line, the Holy Spirit came mightily upon me, and suddenly I was "Acts chapter 2 drunk" (*"these are not drunk as you suppose"*). I continued down the line a little unsteady on my feet, and just as I was about to lay my hands on this one young teenage girl, she grabbed my wrist, looked me in the eyes, and said, "Pray for my pimples!" or something like that. If this prayer request would have happened in America, a young person might have said, "Pray for my zits!" By the time I had come to this young girl, I was so under the power of God with *"joy unspeakable and full of glory"* (1 Pet. 1:8), I almost burst into laughter but smiled at her instead. I thought, *What am I to pray for?* Since I did not know what to say, I just laid my hands on her, and I noticed she was going down under the power of the Lord, so I moved on to the next person. And yet for some reason, I turned and looked back at the young girl on the floor—and I saw her squirm and writhe like a snake! Startled at this display, I thought, *This ain't no zit! What am I to do Lord? Am I to pray and say, Come OUT you spirit of zits, or what?*

Before I heard an answer, I pounced on her and began tackling the snake like a wild warrior commanding the demon to come out of her. Yet the more I gave commands, the more she slithered like a snake. But I was determined not to give up. Then one woman (thank God for the sisters) bent over and whispered in my ear: "Break the neck of the snake!" I thought slowly, repeating each word: *Break the neck of the snake. I didn't know a snake had a neck! Well, OK.* So I reached out for her and found myself grabbing the back of the young girl's neck and said, "In the name of Jesus, and by the shed blood of the Lamb, I break the neck of the snake!" At that command, her arched back immediately relaxed, and with a groan, the evil spirit came out.

Night after night, I preached the Word with great boldness and then gave an altar call. As I would lay my hands on the people, they would be slain in the spirit, many of them manifesting demonic gestures. It was a trip I will never forget. I recall one person's face changed right before me; her countenance turned, and she looked like a monkey. (Some of their ancestors worshipped monkey gods.) Many of them foamed at the mouth when the demon came out. If I hadn't read about these happenings in Jesus' day, I think I would have been a little afraid. For example, an account in Luke 9:39 states, "And behold, a spirit seizes him, and he suddenly cries out; it convulses him so that he foams at the mouth, and it departs from him with great difficulty, bruising him." This all happened because I was ticked off and went on a 40-day fast, and Jesus' anointing came upon me to deliver the people of evil spirits.

It is interesting to note that I did not feel any great anointing during, or even after, the 40-day fast, but when I *needed* that anointing to break the neck of the snake or the demon's hold on the people, God's power was there.

> We do not go by our feelings but by the faith of the Son of God given to us at salvation.

JESUS RETURNS FROM THE WILDERNESS

After Jesus' 40-day fast, Luke 4:14 says, "*Then Jesus returned in the power* [dunamis] *of the Spirit....*" Verse 1 of that same chapter says, "*Then Jesus, being filled with the Holy Spirit....*" It is one thing to be "*filled with*" the Holy Spirit; it is another thing to "*return in the power*" of the Holy Spirit. When Jesus overcame the temptations in the wilderness, He *"returned in the power."* Once the anointing comes upon you, it is necessary to learn how to release that power just like Jesus did.

Jesus' Platform Message

Immediately after the wilderness encounter, in the beginning days of His ministry, Jesus traveled to His hometown of Nazareth, went to the synagogue on the Sabbath day, and sat down. Years ago, I read that the custom in the synagogue is for the visiting rabbi or teacher of the Law to sit in a chair on the left side of the platform while the rabbi or pastor sits on the right side. The chair that was in the middle was reserved only for their long-awaited Messiah. No one had ever sat in that chair.

Jesus takes His rightful place in the synagogue, and the rabbi hands the Book of Isaiah to Jesus. He locates the passage He was to preach, opens His mouth, and speaks with great authority, proclaiming His platform message: *"The Spirit of the Lord is upon Me because He has anointed me…"* (see Luke 4:16-22). Just as He spoke those words, the same anointing that came upon Him at the River Jordan when John baptized Him came upon Him once again! *Because He has anointed me, therefore the Spirit of the Lord is upon me.* He had learned the secret of releasing the anointing, and here it is: *"And they overcame him by the blood of the Lamb and the word of their testimony…"* (Rev. 12:11).

When you *testify* of your salvation, healing, deliverance, or the moment the anointing first came upon you, that *same* anointing will come upon you in the same manner.

73

As Jesus told of His anointing in the River Jordan, that same anointing came on Him again, and He could sense it. Jesus continued His message; *"To preach the gospel to the poor...."* In other words, Jesus told them, "You do not have to be poor anymore." (See 2 Cor. 8:9.) He then went on to say, *"He has sent me to heal the brokenhearted, to proclaim liberty to the captives and recovery of sight to the blind, to set at liberty those who are oppressed; to proclaim the acceptable year of the Lord"* (Luke 4:18-19). (The acceptable year of the Lord is the year of Jubilee; this is now the 40th Jubilee since Jesus was on the earth.)

During the year of Jubilee, which occurred every 50 years, freedom was proclaimed to all people on the Jewish holiday the Day of Atonement (see Lev. 25). When Jesus stood up and read *"to proclaim the acceptable year of the Lord,"* in essence, He was declaring, "I AM your Jubilee! You do not have to wait for another 50 years; I have come to set you free *right now*. You do not have to wait for another 50 years; I have come to heal your bodies *right now*; I have come to save you *right now!*" Imagine Jesus, covered in the anointing, backing into the Messiah's chair, sitting down, and saying, *"Today this Scripture is fulfilled in your hearing."* He said more to them which totally angered them, so in their jealous rage, they rushed at Him to throw Him out of their city—but the anointing oil so covered Him that the Bible says, *"Then passing through the midst of them, He went His way"* (Luke 4:30). He "slipped" right through the crowd to safety.

"Boy, You Have Big Hips!"

I remember years ago when I went into Hong Kong as part of a missionary team, our mission was to "smuggle" Bibles and Bible materials into mainland China. We rendezvoused at a Charismatic church and met with their leaders who approved our team to be "Jesus donkeys" to carry precious material to the underground church. Our contacts gave us white aprons to wear under our skirts to hold the precious items. I put on my white apron under my white cotton skirt. This apron was approximately three feet long and about four feet wide with pockets for the Bible materials and books. I must have had 40 pounds and my very tall female minister companion had at least 60 pounds in her apron.

Before we went to the train station, we spent much time in prayer asking for the Lord's protection as we crossed into mainland China.

As we boarded the train, we had a sense of exhilaration in our spirits that we were doing something illegal and that we would suffer the consequences if caught. But in our hearts, we were at peace, knowing we were in the perfect will of God. The train stopped, and we got in line to go through security screening with armed military guards watching our every move. I walked through the screen tube, my bag came out from the conveyer belt, and I picked it up and started to walk away when a guard commanded me in a gruff voice, pointing in the direction of an interrogation building and nudging me to move toward that building. I thought, "Oh no, Lord, have I been caught?" I struggled with the 40 pounds of weight, literally waddling as if I was seven-months pregnant. Surely, he must see those books! He pointed to a chair, and I struggled to sit as he proceeded to ask me a few questions. Then to my surprise, he motioned for me to leave. As I waddled away, I could feel him staring at me, and I could only assume he must have been thinking, "Boy, those Americans sure have big hips!" Our team went to the designated place, and with precision choreographed by the Holy Spirit, we dropped off our Bible material, making the exchange with the Christian Chinese leaders right under the eyes of the armed guards. Just as Jesus was anointed to walk or slip through the crowd undetected, so we were anointed to slip through security screening and armed guards to put in the hands of the suffering Christians of the underground church of China the precious Bibles and study materials they willingly would give their lives for—just to read the Words of life.

ENDNOTES

1. Charles Finney, quoted in Gwen R. Shaw, *It's Time for Revival* (Jasper, AK: End-Time Handmaidens and Servants), 101.

2. James Strong, *The New Strong's Expanded Exhaustive Concordance of the Bible* (Nashville, TN: Thomas Nelson, 2001); "Hebrew Dictionary," *qavah*, number 6960.

3. Strong, "Greek Dictionary," *Christos*, number 5547.

4. Strong, "Greek Dictionary," *charis*, number 5485.

Chapter 3

DON'T SAY YOU CAN'T
WHEN GOD SAYS YOU CAN!

The following day Jesus wanted to go to Galilee, and He found Philip and said to him, "Follow Me" (John 1:43).

The still, small voice to *come and follow* echoes through the chambers of a longing heart; though the path is not known, the deep desire leads to the narrow way where only the impression of His footsteps are seen. Following closely, you take one step at a time, stretching your gait so your foot can fit snugly into His, not wanting to miss anything He might have for you.

From the time I was born again, in early 1971, I have wanted to see the power of God manifested. I loved the presence of God, so with great anticipation, I would attend every revival meeting, Aglow meeting, Morris Cerullo's anointing service, and Full Gospel Businessmen's gathering just to see God work. With tears of joy, I would watch as each minister would flow with an unseen force—the powerful Holy Spirit—the Wind that fans the flame. While attending one of these meetings, one of the Full Gospel Businessmen's leaders and his wife invited me to their beautiful home for a time of fellowship. After we finished our light lunch, the conversation naturally gravitated to the goodness of the Lord and what He was doing not only in our city of Juneau, Alaska, but also what He was doing in the Church around the world. My quiet and reverential friends, Elmer and Ramona, continued sharing and told me about an upcoming conference called the "World Conference on the Holy Spirit" that was to be in Jerusalem, Israel, the following spring of '74. They told me some of the speakers' names, but since I was a new believer, I had never heard of any of them. Some of them were Jamie Buckingham; Pat Robertson, host of the 700 Club; Costa Deir; J. Rodman Williams, the Presbyterian theologian; Corrie ten Boom; David du Plessis, affectionately called "Mr. Pentecost"; and Kathryn Kuhlman. They seemed quietly excited about this world conference and told me a little about some of the speakers, particularly Miss Kuhlman.

They asked me, "Have you heard of Kathryn Kuhlman?" "No." I said. "Well, they exclaimed, "it is truly amazing that God is using this woman in *such* a great miracle ministry because she wears *makeup!*" (I hardly took note of their comment, but today I chuckle when I think about it, and I am sure they do too.) When they mentioned miracles, I was acutely aware of a quickening in my spirit, and right at that table, I decided that I must go to Jerusalem to see this woman of God being used so mightily in a healing ministry.

In early March, 1974, the Lord supernaturally provided the money that I needed to go to Jerusalem, so I called the travel agent from Logos and booked my ticket for Israel. While boarding the New York jumbo jet for Tel Aviv, I spotted a tall, thin woman, her head and face covered with a beautiful scarf and dark sunglasses, accompanied by Dan Malachuk. (I knew of Mr. Malachuk because of the *Logos Magazine*.) I *somehow* knew this woman was Miss Kuhlman. The Holy Spirit revealed it to me. I stared at her for a long moment and then took a picture of her and boarded our plane. It was a long flight, but the happy singing and praising Christians on the plane made the hours go by quickly.

Once we arrived in Jerusalem, the coordinator assigned our group to buses as we went on tour of the Holy Land. Larry T. and his family were the leaders for our group. One day, as we were walking single-file down the narrow Via Delarosa, where Jesus carried His Cross, a sudden snowstorm began to drop icy cold flakes of wet snow. All the women, including me, were wearing open-toed sandals since we thought the weather was going to be warm in March. Our feet were wet, and we were shivering from the cold. Suddenly, Larry stopped and began to pray, commanding the snow to stop; just as soon as the words left his lips, the snow stopped falling…but only over our heads! I stood in awe as I quietly marveled at the power of God through this young man. After a day of touring, we went back to our hotel room and drifted off to sleep, excited about the following day's activities—we would be attending a healing service where Miss Kuhlman would be ministering.

When I arrived near the auditorium, the crowd had already starting gathering, and slowly they were walking in unity toward the entrance singing, "This is my commandment that you love one another that your joy may be full…." Smiling at the armed Israeli soldiers, we filed through the doors. There were approximately 4,000 of us from 30 different countries, representing every denomination, coming to the city of our God to experience the power of the Holy Spirit. We were the Charismatics—those who believed in the gifts of the Holy Spirit. The last time Jerusalem saw such a crowd was 50 days after Jesus rose from the dead in A.D. 33. They too came from everywhere into the city of David, *"When the Day of Pentecost had fully come; they were all with one accord in one place. And suddenly there came a sound from heaven, as of a rushing mighty wind, and it filled the whole house where they were sitting"* (Acts 2:1-2).

I had found an empty seat as close to the front as possible when I noticed a couple who were short in stature going up and down the aisles introducing themselves to the audience. Soon they came to me and asked, "And where are you from?" "Alaska?" they said with exclamation. It seemed they were intrigued with Alaska, so they stayed and chatted with me for some time. They asked me if I had ever been to one of Miss Kuhlman's crusades, and I told them I had not even heard of Kathryn Kuhlman until a few weeks before I came to this conference. With a startled look on their faces, they told me that they were her head ushers, and they asked me if I would like to sit in one of their seats on the platform! I said, "Yeah, sure." At the time, I did not realize what an honor it was to sit on the platform, but today I cherish those precious moments when I sat just a few feet from Kathryn during her entire lengthy miracle and healing service.

Miss Kuhlman waltzed to the platform in her glass-like slippers and beautiful beige chiffon dress, her skinny arms peeping through. After greeting the crowd and her friends, with a grand sweep of her bony hand, she beckoned Jimmy McDonald to the podium, and he sang to the thrill of the crowd, "His Eye is on the Sparrow." Miss Kuhlman, again with arms outstretched, waved them up and down so we would give Jimmy McDonald more en-thusiastic applause. Then she began to minister the Word. To-ward the end of her short "heart-to-heart talk," she started to weep openly and unashamedly while sharing with us her intimate relationship with the person of the Holy Spirit. Her tears flowed freely down her tilted face as she licked them with her tongue and patted them with her fingers.

Referring to the anointing upon her life, she said, "It costs much, but it is worth the cost." She had my undivided attention. I was captivated with the presence of the Lord upon her life and sat on the edge of my seat as I listened intently to her.

She continued, "It costs everything. If you *really* want to know the price, if you *really* want to know the price, I'll tell you—it will cost you everything!"

After she finished telling her story, the atmosphere suddenly changed from one of silence to the electrifying presence of the great Holy Spirit as He took charge. I looked at her, and her countenance transformed from weeping to an angelic look; with great authority, she suddenly turned toward the balcony and began to call out several diseases by the word of knowledge (see 1 Cor. 12:8). Then she spun around and pointed right at me, and looking me in the eyes, she said, "The Lord has just healed you of a nervous condition. If you *know* you have been healed, I want you to get up here right *now*." I thought something like, "Not on your life!" (She was right; I had a large bald spot on my head from a nervous condition.) By then, I was trembling under the power of God, and I was too afraid to get any closer to her or to this power. What was this power?

When I returned to Juneau, my friend Kathy and I purchased the documentary film on the "World Conference on the Holy Spirit." We showed the film all over Southeast Alaska and gave highlights of each speaker's talks. I *loved* sharing about what had happened in Jerusalem, and I encouraged everyone to go to the next conference. With each viewing of the documentary, a deep desire consumed me to see God's miracles in my life just as I had witnessed in Kathryn's service.

OFF TO BIBLE SCHOOL

When my family was grown up, the Lord put it in my heart to go to Bible School in answer to the call that He placed upon my life when I was 9 years old. I spoke to my husband about this, and we made it a matter of discussion and prayer. For three months, we struggled with this decision, knowing it would mean a time of separation for us. We were childhood sweethearts, and the thought of separation tore at our hearts, but in the end, my husband Mike said I could go. I prayed, asking the Lord where I was to attend Bible School, and while grocery shopping one day, I spotted a Christian magazine near the check-out stand. I bought the magazine, and to my surprise, there was a blurb in the back announcing the Institute of Ministry in Bradenton, Florida. This was the place! I called their office, and they sent me an application in the mail. I quickly filled it out, and soon I was on my way to Gerald Derstine's Bible School. I was never happier in my life! The long hours of study seemed to fly by as each gifted teacher taught us the Word of life. When it came time for my graduation, Mike flew down from Alaska to be with me. During the laying on of hands, my favorite teacher, Tom Nafzinger spoke kind and prophetic words over me, commissioning me into full-time ministry. When it came time to leave the school, I cried uncontrollably, not wanting to leave that anointed place and Glory Blvd., a street I had walked every day talking to the Lord, but it was time to go. The Lord was about to start a new chapter in my life.

So You Wanna' Be a Missionary?

As I was standing in the kitchen, slurping my coffee and rubbing my eyes, I was jarred in my spirit when the phone rang. Who in the world is calling at six in the morning? "Hello," I said in a quiet, raspy voice, hoping no one would answer on the other end. "Hello Sister Flo, this is Sister Henysel!" (Sister Henysel was an old missionary who had come to our Indian village when I was a young girl. After finishing her time of ministry with us, she left our village of Klawock, Alaska, and began a work among the Mexican Indians. Today she is with the Lord.) She had a sound of enthusiasm in her voice as she continued, "I have been working with 35 Mexican pastors just over the border, and I told them about you, and they are wondering if you would agree to come to Mexico and do a five-day crusade in an outdoor arena in September of this year?" (There was a pause.) "Will you come, Sister Flo?"

"Yes." I heard myself saying.

"O Praise the Lord! I will tell them, and we will start a chain fast until the crusade."

"OK Sister Henysel. Bye."

"Bye."

I quietly hung up the phone; then I had this strange foreboding sensation in the pit of my stomach, as if it was full of butterflies gone wild. *O God, what have I done? Lord, I have **never** ever preached before in my life, and I have agreed to do a five-day crusade?*

O Jesus, I moaned. Then, like warm honey running over me, God's reassuring peace pervaded my inner being calming every fear. From that moment, I can honestly say that I never gave the crusade another thought!

1985—OFF TO UGANDA

After that phone call from Sister Hensyel, I left Alaska. I was quietly sitting in a revival service in a church in Canada when the most unexpected thing happened to me. The room was dark because it was a satellite service aired from a large church in Texas. Listening to the speaker, I was captivated with the message when someone gently tapped me on the shoulder and quietly whispered in my ear, "A missionary from Uganda wants to see you after the service." My eyes grew large with aroused curiosity, wondering what this meeting could mean. As soon as the church service adjourned, I quickly left the room, accompanied by a friend, for the pre-arranged meeting place—a nearby McDonald's. We approached the table where a lone woman was sitting. She was a beautiful black woman with a big, friendly smile. My friend introduced her, "This is Florence." (Not her real name.) I sat down, and she immediately broke the silence and told me how she came to know of me. She said someone had given her a cassette tape of my singing. She then asked me to consider going to Uganda with her and her team for their next crusade. *Did you say crusade? Is that where miracles happen?* I wondered. *Yes, of course that is where they happen.* She told me that when she listened to my music cassette, *Rise and Be Healed*, the anointing came on her, and her arms began to tingle, which is what happens when she is ready to lay hands on people for healing and miracles. Then, with strong determination in her voice, she smiled and said, "Would you pray about going to Uganda with us?" I looked at her, immediately dropped my head in reverent prayer, and in the next instant, looked at her with a big smile on my face and said, "Yes! I will go." She looked startled, then laughed, and with that, we agreed to meet in Uganda.

Florence and her international team arrived in Uganda before we did. I traveled from Alaska to Amsterdam and hooked up with my good friend and traveling companion Reba from Oklahoma. (Reba is in Heaven now.) We caught our scheduled flight to Africa, enjoying each other's company along the way. When we arrived at the Christian compound where the team was staying, Reba and I quickly unpacked. A driver came for us and drove us to a large building where 1,000 Ugandan ministers had been fasting and praying for a week. When I walked into the building, the room was more than hot from the temperature outside—it was hot with God's fiery Presence! I sat near the front, absorbed in listening to one minister after another take the microphone, confessing sins of commission and omission. Some of them wailed as they confessed, saying, "I heard people being tortured, but I refused to do anything about it." They were talking about their past dictator, a tyrant who had murdered hundreds of thousands of Christians and political prisoners in the short years of his oppressive rule.

> The Christian leaders said that if we had only acted, if we had only prayed and fasted, this could not have happened to the extreme that it did.

When the confessions stopped, we all went to the altar and fell on the dusty floor on our faces, crying out to the only One who could turn the "pearl of Africa" back to the glory she once knew. When the people quieted before the Lord, one by one, the ministers stood up to leave. I too left the building; walking out into the bright sunlight, I squinted, looking for a familiar face so I could get a ride back to the compound. Mucasa, one of the Ugandan team members came to me, and we made light conversation waiting for the rest of the ministers to show up. Then he turned to me, looked into my eyes, and said in a passionate voice, "Sister *Flow*, we are so happy you have come to Uganda when so many missionaries are afraid to come for fear of their lives... but *you* came. Thank you Sister *Flow*."

When he first starting speaking to me, I gave him my big, warm missionary smile, nodding when he thanked me for coming to his country, but as he commended me for coming "when so many...fear for their lives," my big smile slowly dropped, and I looked at him with anguish: "Mucasa, what do you mean, fear for their lives?" He looked at me in puzzlement and told me about their leader who slaughtered so many of his people. He told me that they are killing people even now, and that there is a 6 P.M. nightly curfew. And he told me of the nightly voodoo drums. I said to him, with great emotion, "Mucasa, if my husband would have known about this—that there is still much killing going on—he would *never* have allowed me to come!" (I felt trapped. So you want to be a missionary?)

With that, we drove back to the compound in silence, and I fell on my cot exhausted from the flight and the day's intercessions. As I lay there, contemplating what Mucasa said to me earlier that day, I fell asleep to the sound of those distant voodoo drums with their chanting beat and the blasting of AK-47s in the next neighborhood. Later we would come face-to-face with those AK-47s.

By the third day, a sudden mysterious illness struck my precious friend and traveling companion Reba, and she became quite ill and bedfast. As I was lying on my cot, I heard Reba groan; I looked at her. She was arching her back, and the grimace of pain on her face made me jump up quickly and run to her bedside. I laid hands on her, praying a panic prayer over her, but of course, she continued to groan. The leader of our team heard the commotion and joined me in prayer, but we did not see any change in Reba. Then a tall, slenderly-built young prophet from another African country came in "cool as a cucumber" and laid his big hands on her.

Unlike our panicky prayers, he quietly and calmly said, "I command the spirit of death to leave and the life of God to flow into you now in the name of Jesus." And as quickly as she had arched her back, she slowly and quietly laid back on the cot, her blue fingernails turning a pale pink. She was going to be all right. When the crisis was over, our leader Florence told Reba to get dressed, and she and our driver Jeffrey drove her to the hospital, where the doctor diagnosed her with some terrible disease. Florence told him that it was impossible for her to have contracted this disease because she had just arrived in the country. After bringing her back to the compound, Florence decided that, for her own welfare, Reba must return to Oklahoma.

The next day, Reba packed, and Denise, another team member from the U.S., and I accompanied our friend to the Ugandan airport with Jeffrey our driver. After we said our tearful goodbyes, we headed back to our compound. As we were passing the old Entebbe Airport, Denise told me that it was no longer an airport but a military compound. I asked, "Is this where the Jewish raid took place?" They said yes, so I quickly took several pictures of this famous place. It was definitely something to write home about.

Briefly, here is the story of Entebbe. It was in June, 1976, that terrorists hijacked an Air France plane carrying over 200 passengers, forcing the captain to alter course and eventually land at Uganda's Entebbe Airport. With the tacit approval of President

Idi Amin, the terrorists held the Jewish passengers hostage and threatened them with death if the Israeli government did not comply with their captor's demands to release 53 Palestinians held in Israeli prisons. The world held its breath as the hours and minutes to the deadlines set by the terrorists ticked by. Then, elite Israeli troops flew from Israel, undetected for hundreds of miles, landed at Entebbe to fight a battle that lasted about an hour, freeing their people, and flew out of the country before Idi Amin could arrive with his army to stop them. I just *had* to have photos of this airport.

While driving from Entebbe Airport, I was still feeling sadness about Reba's departure when all of a sudden a man with a machine gun stepped out from the brush and stood in the middle of the highway, forcing us to come to a screeching halt. He slowly walked around the front of the car to the back seat where I was sitting, motioning me to roll down the window. Jeffrey quietly said with a forceful command, "*Pray* in tongues *now* and bind the spirit of greed!" We started praying immediately. I had taken off my sunglasses so he could see my eyes if he asked me questions. I wanted him to know I was speaking the truth and had nothing to hide. He motioned with the end of the AK-47 in my face to get out of the car.

Denise whispered, "Grab your sunglasses!" I thought, *Grab my sunglasses, why? Why does she want me to take my glasses, to prove I was never here?* All kinds of crazy thoughts started to go through my mind. I knew I must quiet those thoughts. *No fear, show no fear.*

I got out of the car. He demanded, his reddened eyes staring at me with great contempt, "Open your purse!" I thought, *Oh God, he is going to see my camera; then he will develop the film and see I took pictures of Entebbe, and he will think I am a spy and kill me…O Jesus, help me!* He looked in my large purse and then told me to get back in the car. With my hands now shaking, I opened the car door and almost jumped in.

Now it was Denise's turn. Jeffrey whispered with a sound of fear in his voice that was infecting the atmosphere inside the vehicle, "Bind the spirit of greed!"

Denise was the treasurer of our group; she had thousands in Ugandan money, which really amounted to little in American dollars, but in a war-torn country, it was their lifeblood. I started to pray hard. He growled at her, "Give me the money!" The demon in him must have revealed to him that she was carrying the money. They were both about the same height.

Denise was an ex-cop turned preacher-woman. When he told her to give him the money, she retorted, "NO!" I thought, *De-neeece…give it to him!* Now they were standing toe-to-toe, and like two boxers, they gave each other this non-verbal communication. Then it was spirit-to-spirit, and Christ in Denise was stronger, much stronger, than the demon in him, so he slowly complied, lowered his AK-47 in submission, and waved his gun motioning her to leave.

She walked with confidence back around the front of the vehicle and got in, and we quietly drove away. After two long minutes, I asked Jeffrey, "Was that smart of Denise to do that, Jeffrey?"

"No," he replied with a shaken voice, "but she did not have time to think. She spoke by the Holy Ghost." He then added, "There were some men who were traveling on this same road last week, and they refused to give up their money, so more men with machine guns came from the brush and surrounded the vehicle, pulled the men out, gave them the boot (kicked them), and they were dead-on-arrival at the hospital."

After a brief silence, I said, "Denise, *if I ever* come back to Uganda, I want you to come with me."

ANOINTED TO PREACH

The next morning I awoke to the sound of the breakfast bell—except it was not a bell but a woman beating a drum. We quickly went to the bathroom to take our daily shower—except there was not a showerhead but a low spigot on the wall. I turned it on and let it run for a long time, hoping warm water would eventually come out, but only frigid water fell to the floor, splashing my legs. I cupped my hands, filled them with the cold water, threw it on my chest, and gasped as the icy water shocked me fully awake. The last time I experienced that was when I lived in my Indian village as a child. As I walked down the path to the breakfast hall, there were two large vultures humped over on a wire, their eyes slowly following me as if waiting for *their* breakfast. It sent a shiver through me until I remembered that they only like to pick on dead things.

Feeling fully alive in Jesus, I went to the breakfast table, and Florence introduced me to the team. After our breakfast of plantains and other Ugandan food, we prayed and headed to the grassy area where the outdoor crusade was to begin. On the ground sat thousands of people watching our every move. Some of them had a light in their eyes, but most of them had a dark countenance that only the light of Christ could change. Florence went to the platform and opened the meeting with prayer. The enthusiastic music accompanied by dancing set the meeting in motion. When it came to my turn, Florence called me to the platform to testify and to sing, "The Wind is Blowin' Again." The crowd seemed to enjoy that song as they danced to the beat of the music.

Then our main speaker, Archbishop Victor Onigbo from Nigeria, along with his interpreter Robert Kyanja, went to the platform and preached the Word of God with a combined power I had not witnessed since the '74 Jerusalem conference. With tremendous authority, Brother Victor rebuked demon spirits by commanding them to come out, and I watched with great awe and wonder as the people were healed by the miraculous power of God. Hour after hour, day after day, I sat in rapt attention on the platform as one after another were healed. This went on for about three weeks, and at the end of the crusade, we were all physically tired.

Before leaving for our trip back home, Florence called a special meeting just for our team. She asked Brother Victor to teach us. While he was sharing on the anointing, my body suddenly felt numb, and my head starting nodding from a lack of sleep. When Brother Victor saw that, he said with a stern voice, "Isn't that right, Sister Flo?" I looked at him sheepishly and quietly apologized for being tired. He gave me that look as if to say, that is no excuse, Flo. When he turned his head to look at the other team members, I took my leave quickly and quietly slipped out of the room. I crawled in bed and instantly fell into a deep sleep. All of a sudden, Florence was rudely shaking me out of my slumber.

"Sister Flo, Sister Flo, you *must* come, the power of God is falling on the team."

"No, please Florence, I want to sleep. Besides, I have my pajamas on."

"Never mind," she said. "You can put your robe on."

Reluctantly I obeyed God's authority, and I put my robe on, shuffling behind her as she forced me back into the meeting. As we opened the door, I felt that same electrifying Presence of the

Holy Spirit, and I immediately stood erect, now fully awake. The first thing I did was quickly access the situation, my eyes darting from person to person. Then my gaze stopped at Brother Victor as I watched him take small quick steps toward a young Canadian couple and ask them, "What do you want the Lord to do?"

"We want the anointing."

With that, Brother Victor threw his arms in the air, reached out, and laid his hands on them. They immediately began to shake violently under the power of God. When he was finished, he turned around with that wide-eyed look that I have come to know, which indicates that Brother Victor is under a heavy anointing, and said, "Who's next?"

Florence pointed to me and said, "She is!"

I protested loudly, "No, Florence is." Florence gave me that look, and the Lord told me to submit, so I walked over to the now empty chair, and he came close to me.

"What do you want from the Lord?" I thought, why do ministers always ask me that question? I felt like saying, why don't you give me your best shot, but I heard these words coming out of my mouth, "I want to preach!"

He looked at me with a surprised look and shouted, "You *are* preaching!"

I said, "I am *not* preaching; I am testifying and singing. I want to preach!" With that, he started to come toward me, ready to lay his hands on me, when without warning, he stopped and then stepped backward, his hands springing into mid air as if he touched something very hot.

He shouted an order, "Stand on your feet, for the Lord says He will anoint you Himself." All I could do was meekly obey as I stood trembling in God's Presence. "Lift your hands!" he directed. As I lifted my arms in total surrender, I started doing the "Pentecostal shaking" (something I usually do not do), and he shouted again, "*There it is,* the anointing is coming down on you. It is around your heart. He is giving you a heart of flesh. *There it is,* around your legs…" Before he could finish, down I went, slain by the Power of God, with no catcher. I do not know how long I lay on that cold cement floor; when I finally got up I did not *feel* any different, but I knew *something* had happened to me.

When I was preparing to go back to the United States, I went to speak with Brother Victor privately and said to him, "Oh, by the way, I am going to Mexico to preach a five-day crusade. *What do I preach at a crusade, Brother Victor?*"

He looked at me with a quizzical look, and then with great tenderness, he said in a whisper, "Just tell them about Jesus." I thought I could do that, so with that simple instruction, I headed back home to Alaska.

THE MEXICAN CRUSADE

The Holy Spirit gently nudged me awake. "Today is the day; today you head to Mexico to do your first crusade (O Hallelujah!)." I stretched out of a fetal position, rolled out of bed, and packed enough clothes for the five-day crusade. In my quiet time on the plane, the Holy Spirit directed my thoughts about the crusade. Thoughts once locked away by Him these past months—now released—flooded me with questionings. *I wonder what the Lord is going to do in Mexico.* As I mused, I pulled my Bible from my carry-on bag and asked the Lord to speak to me. I asked Him,

"What are *You* going to do at this crusade?" As if to say, this was *Your* idea and whatever happens will be *Your* fault. As I was waiting for Him to respond, my thoughts went back to an earlier conference I hosted in Alaska. (I was only the host.) At the height of the powerful outpouring, He said to me in that still small voice that I *know* is the Holy Spirit, "Flo, if you will not take the glory for the victory, I will not credit you with the defeat." That sounded like a good deal to me. "Yes, Lord," I whispered to Him.

My thoughts slowly returned to Mexico, and then He led me to Exodus 6:1: "*Then the Lord said unto Moses, 'Now shalt thou see what I will do to Pharaoh….'*" I said under my breath smiling, "I *know* what you did to Pharaoh. You spoiled him with signs, wonders, and miracles, yes, miracles! O glory!" With that, I settled back into my seat with an inner confidence in this mighty God that I served.

After I arrived in Arizona, Sister Henysel arranged for me to meet my Spanish interpreter. She told me to give my testimony, and he would interpret. She listened to my Puerto Rican interpreter to find out how well he could interpret, and after listening a few moments said, "He'll do." Sister Henysel gave us instructions to pray for the first evening's meeting, that it would not rain; they had been in a drought, and when the ground cannot contain the rain, a flash flood can quickly develop. We agreed to pray. However, before we went our separate ways, my interpreter said that the Lord told him to give me a prophetic word, "*As I was with my servant Moses, so shall I be with you.*" When I heard those words, my heart flooded with joy as I went to my "prayer closet" to intercede for the evening's service. While in prayer, I asked the Lord, "What do you want me to preach?" He said to preach from the last chapters in the Book of

Matthew. I turned there and began to read the account of Christ's trial and crucifixion.

I prayed in the Spirit's language (tongues) and read Matthew 27-28 for hours.

When it was time to head to the crusade, I felt strangely engulfed in peace about what I was going to preach and the tremendous honor it was to bring His Good News to the Mexican people. When we arrived at the stadium in Mexico, thousands of people had already gathered and were waiting in the bleachers with great anticipation for the meeting to start. Sister Henysel introduced me to all 35 pastors. I greeted them, and they treated me with such respect, as if I were somebody *great*. While the last-minute preparations were underway, it still never occurred to me to tell those 35 pastors, or Brother and Sister Henysel, that I had *never preached one message before, let alone at a crusade with thousands in attendance.* Somehow, it was not important to me, and I had the impression it was not important to the Holy Spirit either.

Finally, the meeting started. With instruments blaring through the sound system, we sang old-time Pentecostal songs with vigorous enjoyment as only Mexican people can sing. When it came time for the preaching of the Word, the MC for the meeting said with great emphasis on each syllable, *"Pa-leeeez, welcome, in-ter-national e-van-ge-list Floooo Ell-errrs!"* With that, the people clapped and roared, but I was so in the Spirit (without fully recognizing the fact) that I hardly noticed the noise; I was totally focused on the Lord. My interpreter and I walked briskly across the dry field, up the stairs onto the makeshift platform, and up to the podium. The very second that I grabbed the microphone, the power of God struck me like a bolt of lightning coursing through my body!

To my utter surprise, I shouted with great authority, "Open your Bible to Matthew 27!" *Is this my voice I am hearing? It does not even resemble me. This must be the great Holy Spirit preaching through me!* In perfect unison, my interpreter stayed with me. Every word I said, he said, even to the very inflection of my voice. Every action I did, he did. I was now on a roll. When I got to the part of Jesus' crucifixion, dark ominous clouds began to form and then rolled overhead as the wind began howling and whipping the dry sand into the air. What was happening? Huge drops of rain suddenly began to fall, which quickly turned into a downpour soaking the wooden platform and all the instruments. Another powerful wind came again, but this time it whipped my notes from my Bible, off the podium, and into the air. While my interpreter was speaking, I had the realization that I was holding a live mic in my hand connected to an electrical outlet. My thoughts were racing as I watched the crowd becoming agitated. I knew they were about to leave if the rain continued to downpour.

Then I felt this righteous anger rising up inside of me. (At that moment, I did not know that it was the gift of faith in operation.)

I looked down at my wet Bible, trying to find the Scripture where I had left off. I found it, and I opened my mouth to read the Scripture, when out of my mouth these words came instead, "In the name of *Jesus*, I come against you by the shed blood of the Lamb, and I rebuke you satan and command this wind and rain to stop *now*!" It did! And I did! Oh, Glory to God! The people gasped in awe, but I think I was definitely more surprised than they were! I then moved into the most important part of the service; I gave the altar call for people to surrender their lives to Jesus, and 500 people came forward that night.

After we led the people in the sinner's prayer, I called on the 35 pastors and asked them to help me pray for the sick. We laid hands on those precious Mexican people, and miracle after miracle occurred as the Holy Spirit flowed through us. Women came to me and said through Sister Henysel, who was my interpreter, "Tell this woman I want the anointing like she has."

Sister Henysel would tell them, "It is not *her* anointing; it is the Lord doing the miracles." However, I do not think we could convince them. They kept crowding around me, but I knew better than any of them that I could not have done any of this.

I knew it had happened because the pastors and intercessors had fasted and prayed for months. The wind of God caused those 500 precious people who were once in darkness to come into His light. *He* opened their blind eyes; *He* did those miracles; *He* healed those cataracts; *He* caused that lame man to walk. Jesus did it all. He was the miracle worker.

When the crusade was over, I went home rejoicing over all those who were saved and healed despite the persecution I encountered from the religious devils while in Mexico. To me, it was worth it all. After the crusade was over, Sister Henysel told me that the religious leaders were preaching over the local radio telling the people not to come to my crusade because I was "practicing black magic." I am so glad I knew nothing of this until later because I know it would have hindered me. Not everyone will be thrilled when your meetings break out into a revival.

 If you cannot handle persecution, rejection, lies, or critics you should not go into the ministry. Remember when Simeon picked up the Baby Jesus and blessed Him in the Book of Luke 2:34-35: *"Then Simeon blessed them, and said to Mary His mother, 'Behold, this Child is destined for the fall and rising of many in Israel, and for a sign which will be spoken against....'"*

After that crusade, I witnessed a few miracles and some signs and wonders in my ministry, but the Lord, in His wisdom, lifted that power off of me; that is, I experienced it to a lesser degree.

I believe He did that to me *and* for me because of my immaturity, because the same power that opens blind eyes can blind your eyes...to your own pride.

Do you recall when Elijah threw his miracle mantle on Elisha? (See First Kings 19:19.) Well, if you remember, he took the mantle back!

It was not until Elisha was ready, prepared, and mature that Elijah was free to leave the earth and go up into Heaven. Then the miracle mantle fell.

When Elisha went to pick up the mantle, he had to bend over low in humility to pick it up. I believe the Lord drops His miracle mantle on us to see if we really want to pay the price to move in *that* anointing. Once we have passed our tests, and endured the dealings of God, He will place it back on us—in the place of His choosing and in His timing.

WHAT IS IN YOUR HAND?

Through each individual, a special anointing, a unique expression of Jesus is shown to the world. Some will move in mighty power; some in signs, wonders, and miracles; some as teachers; and some as helpers. The Holy Spirit has a unique preparation for your unique calling and ministry, and no matter where He has placed you in the Body of Christ, signs should follow everywhere you go. Mark 16:17 says, *"And these signs shall follow those who believe…."* When God called Moses, He had to do a deep work in him before he was ready to lead God's people out of bondage.

"Before the Lord qualified Moses, He had to disqualify him," my precious friend Art said when he described the process God took Moses through as preparation for his leadership. For 40 years, on the backside of the desert, God did a work in Moses' life that only *He* could do as He stripped him of all pride and shaped him into a deliverer who would set his people free from bondage. Alone in that desert, Moses not only faced the elements and wild animals, but he also had a face-to-face encounter with *Himself.* Only in quiet moments, when we allow the Lord to go deep into what we have been hiding, will we be fit for His work. Those are painful moments of repentance—but they are necessary if we are to become what He has determined for our destiny and calling.

When the process was over, God called Moses to come before Him so He could commission him into full-time ministry. Moses began to argue with God because he did not feel adequate for the job, thinking *he* would have to do the miracles, *he* would have to be the deliverer, and *he* would have to bring his people out of Pharaoh's bondage.

He protested to the Lord, not realizing that his sense of inadequacy *was* his qualification.

And Moses answered and said, "But, behold, they will not believe me, nor hearken unto my voice: for they will say, the Lord hath not appeared unto thee." And the Lord said unto him, "What is that in thine hand?" And he said, "A rod" (Exodus 4:1-2 KJV).

To restore his lost confidence and equip him for his ministry, God gave Moses final proofs of his calling—two signs that He was *with* him and that *He* would be the One to deliver the people:

And He said, "Cast it on the ground." So he cast it on the ground, and it became a serpent; and Moses fled from it. Then the Lord said to Moses, "Reach out your hand and take it by the tail" (and he reached out his hand and caught it, and it became a rod in his hand)....Furthermore the Lord said to him, "Now put your hand in your bosom." And he put his hand in his bosom, and when he took it out, behold, his hand was leprous, like snow. And He said, "Put your hand in your bosom again." So he put his hand in his bosom again, and drew it out of his bosom, and behold it was restored like his other flesh. "Then it will be, if they do not believe you, nor heed the message of the first sign, that they may believe the message of the latter sign" (Exodus 4:3-8).

The two signs God gave to Moses are the same signs Jesus has given to the church. When Moses picked the snake up by the tail and it became a rod in his hand, the Lord was showing him that he had power over demons; when he put his hand in his bosom and his leprous hand became whole, the Lord was showing him that he had healing power in his hands. Jesus said in Matthew 10:7-8, *"As you go, preach, saying, 'The kingdom of heaven is at hand* [in your hand].' *Heal the sick, cleanse the lepers, raise the dead, cast out demons. Freely you have received, freely give."*

If the Lord came to you and asked, "What is that in *your* hand?" Some of you would answer, "I dunno!" I said, "What is that in *your* hand?" "O nuth-in!" Most of us do not feel qualified to do the impossible tasks the Lord is asking of us. Nevertheless, because He lives in us, He has qualified us.

> As we obey each command and *step out in faith*, the Holy Spirit will flow through us. Some things you are not yet ready for, but start where you are, where your faith level is. With each step you take in obedience to His commands, miracles will happen—one small miracle leading to a bigger miracle. As you step out, you will find that the Lord will work with you as He did with the early disciples. *"And they went out and preached everywhere, the* **Lord working with them** *and confirming the word through the accompanying signs"* (Mark 16:20).

Chapter 4

GLORY THAT EXCELS

But if the ministry of death, written and engraved on stones, was glorious, so that the children of Israel could not look steadily at the face of Moses because of the glory of his countenance, which glory was passing away, how will the ministry of the Spirit not be more glorious? For if the ministry of condemnation had glory, the ministry of righteousness exceeds much more in glory. For even what was made glorious had not glory in this respect, because of the glory that excels (2 Corinthians 3:7-10).

"Mike, Mike, I can't see!" I cried out. "Please Mike, help me, I can't see!" My serene early morning devotions turned into a panic. I had just returned from a long ministry trip to Asia where we had experienced a glorious move of God with signs, wonders, and a few miracles. Despite coming home exhausted, I was relaxed and basking in the Lord's presence. It was around 6 a.m. when I slipped out of bed so I would not disturb my husband. I quietly sneaked down the stairs, made myself a cup of coffee, and snuggled into a comfortable chair to read. I opened my Bible to Revelation 4 and read,

> *After these things I looked, and behold, a door standing open in heaven. And the first voice, which I heard, was like a trumpet speaking with me, saying, "Come up here, and I will show you things which must take place after this." Immediately I was in the Spirit; and behold, a throne set in heaven, and One sat on the Throne. And He who sat there was like a jasper..."* (Revelation 4:1-3).

As I was reading, I noticed the words began to fade and become a blur. I blinked several times, but that did not help. I continued reading. Then to my astonishment, the words slowly faded away until I could no longer see. When Mike heard the alarm in my voice, he bounded out of bed and ran down the stairs.

"Honey, what's wrong?" he asked with more than a little concern in his voice.

"I can't see Mike," I cried out in terror. Mike is sensitive to the Holy Spirit, so he quickly processed the situation. He put his strong arms around me, held me for a brief reassuring moment, and said, "Let's go upstairs." He guided me slowly, gently up the stairs and made me lay on the bed where he held me for about 30 minutes until my vision slowly returned. That happened in the early '90s.

I had to have a biblical answer to find out what happened to me, so I began to study the Scriptures on the subject of the glory of God. The Word declares that we are given *grace for grace* (see John 1:16); we go from *faith to faith* (see Rom. 1:16-17) and from *glory to glory* (see 2 Cor. 3:18). I had experienced a measure of the glory in past meetings, so maybe this was another measure of His Presence. I wondered.

> *Now the Lord is the Spirit; and where the Spirit of the Lord is, there is liberty. But we all, with unveiled face, beholding as in a mirror the glory of the Lord, are being transformed into the same image from glory to glory, just as by the Spirit of the Lord* (2 Corinthians 3:17-18).

We believers behold the glory of the Lord by His abiding Presence in the Word, and it is a transforming glory. In my view, a transcendent glory is intensifying in these last days as the Holy Spirit is doing His deep work of sanctification so that He might present to the heavenly Father a glorious Church: *"That He might present the church to Himself in glorious splendor, without spot, wrinkle, or any such things [that she might be holy and faultless]"* (Eph. 5:27 AMP).

The Lord said in the Old Testament, *"And there I will meet with the children of Israel, and the tabernacle shall be sanctified by My glory. So I will consecrate that tabernacle..."* (Exod. 29:43-44). We are now *that* tabernacle of God that He is setting apart for His own use and His own purpose, and our total consecration to Him shows divine ownership. As we totally yield to Him, He floods our "tabernacle" with His glory. In the Bible, it tells us that the Lord filled the upper room (see Acts 2:2; 4:31), the tabernacle (see Exod. 40:34), the temple (see 2 Chron. 5:14; 7:1), a prison (see Acts 16:26), and a mountain (see Exod. 19:18) with His glory. So if He can fill a building, a prison, and a mountain, He can fill us with that same glory: *"Christ in me, the hope of glory"* (Col. 1:27).

In the Old Testament, the word glory in Hebrew comes from the word *kabowd*, translated "weight, splendor, copiousness, glory." In the New Testament, the word for glory is *doxa*, which means "dignity, glory, honor, praise, worship."[1] In Second Corinthians 4:17, Paul said, *"light affliction"* produces an *"exceeding and eternal weight of glory."* Paul first understood this "weight" when he encountered Jesus Christ on the road to Damascus.[2] He said,

> *I saw a light from heaven, brighter than the sun, shining around me and those who journeyed with me. And when we all had fallen to the ground, I heard a voice speaking to me…So I said, "Who are you Lord?" And He said, "I am Jesus whom you are persecuting. But rise and stand on your feet; for I have appeared unto you for this purpose, to make you a minister and a witness…"* (Acts 26:12-18).

When the glory of God showed up in the Presence of Jesus, no one could stand under that power.

Not only Paul but also all the men with him were slain under the power of God…but only Paul was changed. I am not so much interested in whether you're getting slain in the Spirit but in whether you're changed when you get up.

Paul's encounter with Jesus had purpose: *"…for I have appeared unto you for this purpose…to open their eyes, in order to turn them from darkness to light, and from the power of Satan to God, that they may receive forgiveness of sins…"*(Acts 26:15,18).

In Acts 9:7-9, the Bible continues with the story of Paul (Saul) after he saw the brilliant light of Jesus and was blinded by the glory: *"Then Saul arose from the ground, and when his eyes were opened he saw no one. But they led him by the hand and brought him to Damascus. And he was three days without sight…"*

This same *glory manifested* in Second Chronicles 5 when the sanctified priests carried the ark into Solomon's temple to the Most Holy Place, under the wings of the cherubim. As the priests began to blow their trumpets and the Levites began to sing,

> *"For the Lord is good, for His mercy endures forever,"…the house of the Lord was filled with a cloud, so that the priests could not continue ministering because of the cloud; for the glory of the Lord filled the house of God* (2 Chronicles 5:13-14).

The Amplified Bible indicates that the 120 *"priests could not stand"* upright because the manifest glory was so thick and heavy. Just as Saul (or Paul) was slain on the road to Damascus, the same glory Presence also overcame these priests. When the priests recovered, Solomon continued with the inauguration service dedicating the temple to the Lord. When he finished praying, the Bible says the glory came again, but the weight of it greatly increased so he priests could not even enter the temple!

> *When Solomon had finished praying…the glory of the Lord filled the temple. And the priests could not enter the house of the Lord, because the glory of the Lord had filled the Lord's house. When all the children of Israel saw how the fire came down, and the glory of the Lord on the temple, they bowed their faces to the ground…* (2 Chronicles 7:1-3).

GLORY CLOUD IN ZIMBABWE

In 1986, my friend Sheila and I attended Reinhard Bonnke's first "Fire Conference," which he held in Harare, Zimbabwe. The conference had one main purpose—to spread the fire of revival to thousands of Africans and evangelists. Christian leaders from around the world attended this gathering. Reverend Bonnke labeled this meeting the "occasion of the century." The organizer told us that if all the applicants who wanted to attend this conference were accepted, evangelists from around the world would have filled the streets of Harare. We felt honored to be among those chosen to attend.

After Sheila, I, and 35,000 other people trekked through the deep African mud to get to the largest tent in the world, we found our assigned seats near the front. We were thrilled to be a part of this first-ever "Fire Conference," and we were fully expecting the fire of God to fall. But the glory of the Lord came in a way we never expected. It was glorious to watch as, night after night, the power of God would fall upon the thousands as miracle after miracle occurred. Nevertheless, the greatest sign and wonder happened during the altar call when Evangelist Bonnke gave his salvation message, and I literally saw thousands of precious Africans stampeding to the front of the tent, almost knocking down some camera operators to give their lives to Jesus. (I thought, *Someday Lord, I will see this in America.*)

After he led them in a sinner's prayer, the people nearest the front began to scream, "Look, Look!" They pointed with their fingers turned upward as the American team lifted up their video cameras to catch the phenomenon on tape. I looked up in the direction they were pointing, and I saw billows and billows of blue smoke swirling at the pointed top of the tent. I immediately thought, *They [the new converts] must have stirred up the sawdust from the ground! Then I had a second thought, No dummy, how could sawdust be twirling up there...that's smoke...that's the Glory*

Cloud! O Jesus, O Jesus! It was beautiful, a dark turquoise in color, and swirling like blue clouds. I have never witnessed anything quite like that.

Then Brother Bonnke gave another call, this time for healing. Just as the words of command to be healed came out of his mouth, the power of God hit a man who had been brought in on a stretcher by four friends (just like in Luke 5:17-25). This man, overcome with joy, ran up the stairs onto the platform, and with hands uplifted, praised the Lord in a loud voice. Then the people started yelling again, "Look! Look!" pointing to the bright blue Glory Cloud that again appeared swirling at the top of the 35,000-seat tent. I did not have a video camera, but the memory, forever etched in my heart, remains vividly to this day. Later in the week, I had the opportunity to sing "Sweet Anointing" in that glorious tent just before Bonnke preached.

> *Arise, shine; for your light has come! And the glory of the Lord is risen upon you. For behold, the darkness shall cover the earth, and deep darkness the people; but the Lord will arise over you, and His glory will be seen upon you. The Gentiles shall come to your light...* (Isaiah 60:1-3).

MOSES SEES GOD'S GLORY

Moses boldly sought the Lord because he greatly desired to see God's glory: *"Please, show me Your glory"* (Exod. 33:18). God tenderly answered Moses, *"I will make all my goodness pass before you...Here is the place by Me, and you shall stand on the rock...I will put you in the cleft of the rock...then I will take away My hand, and you shall see My **back**..."* (Exod. 33:19-23). If you do a word study on the word *back*, you will find that it means "back, hinder parts, behind, backward."[3] God told Moses He would show him His goodness. How can you see goodness? You cannot. You can see the result of goodness, but you cannot see goodness and mercy. Could it be that Moses saw Jesus' back? When he saw that shredded back, ripped open to the bone, he saw God's goodness and compassion. I cannot imagine the degree of agony that Moses experienced if it was Jesus' back that he saw. The glory of that moment was life changing. That glory so reflected on Moses' face that he had to cover himself.

It so humbled him that he did not want anyone looking at him.

He wanted them to look upon the Savior. Anyone, like Moses, can cry out for more of God. He will manifest Himself to you if you desire more of Him. Moreover, when He manifests His glory, it will change or transform you into a person of great mercy and compassion. If Jesus showed you His back, it would leave you completely undone. No one could witness such a scene and not be transformed into His divine attributes. Second Peter 1:2-4 says,

> Grace and peace be multiplied to you in the knowledge of God and of Jesus our Lord, as His divine power has given to us all things that pertain to life and godliness, through the knowledge of Him who called us by glory and virtue, by which have been given to us exceedingly great and precious promises, that through these you may be partakers of the divine nature...."

Psalm 8:5 tells us that He has crowned us with *"glory and honor."* That honor is beauty, excellence, and magnificence. Jesus does not see us as we see ourselves. When He looks at us, He looks with eyes of tender love.

THE FIRE AND THE GLORY

The prophet Jeremiah said, *"Because you speak this word, behold, I will make My words in your mouth fire"* (Jer. 5:14).

 When a minister reads and studies the Word and fasts and prays, a fire begins to burn in his or her spirit; and when he or she stands up to minister, the fire consumes whatever is not of the Lord in the hearts and lives of the people of God.

There are times when the Lord can make the words of your mouth flow with supernatural strength. In Psalm 45:1, the psalmist said, *"My heart is overflowing with a good theme...my tongue is the pen of a ready writer."* When that happens, it feels like you are writing upon the tablets of people's hearts. There is no substitute for the fire of God in the mouth of God's messengers. My good friend Brother Victor from Nigeria told me of a time when he was ministering in a large field, doing an outdoor crusade in his beloved Africa, when the fire of God came out of his mouth. He said he did not intend to say this, but while preaching the Word, these words came out. He shouted, "There is a witch within the sound of my voice, and you have been cursing this meeting. The Lord says if you do not repent, all your teeth will fall out!" He said he did not miss a beat but kept right on preaching. When he was finished, he gave the altar call, and while he was ministering to the people, a woman came screaming into the meeting, running up the field to the ministry area with blood gurgling out of her mouth. They led her in a sinner's prayer and cast devils out of her. She told them that she was the witch who was cursing the meeting. Apparently, all her teeth had fallen out!

Some years later Brother Victor told me he had seen the woman once again, and I asked him quickly, "Did her teeth grow back?"

He replied with a smile on his face, "No, she remains toothless, but she is still serving the Lord!"

TREMBLING IN THE GLORY

Daniel of old began to fast and pray and sought the face of the Lord for 21 days. During those days, a battle took place in the heavenlies where demonic forces kept the angel of the Lord from breaking through to bring an answer to Daniel's prayers. When the angel came to Daniel, he put his hand on Daniel, who began to tremble uncontrollably. Daniel 10:10 says, *"Suddenly, a hand touched me, which made me tremble on my knees and on the palms of my hands."* His knees were having "fellowship" as they banged together. Then the angel tells him, *"Do not fear..."* (Dan. 10:12). If I saw an angel from Heaven manifest in front of me, I think I would fear too. In the glory, angels surround you and minister to you. I have sensed their presence many times, and when they come, I too tremble. While in intense worship, sometimes the angels will come to see who you are worshipping. If you are praying in your heavenly language and angels are present, you can begin to pray in their language. Paul the apostle said in First Corinthians 13:1, *"Though I speak with the tongues of men and of angels...."*

ANGEL WINGS

Many times in the glory, you can sense an unusual presence of the Lord or the presence of angelic beings. Ezekiel said in 3:12-14, *"I heard behind me a great thunderous voice: 'Blessed is the glory of the Lord from His place.' I also heard the noise of the wings of the living creatures that touched one another, and the noise of the wheels*

116

beside them...the hand of the Lord was strong upon me." The first time I heard the sound of angels was when I was first born again. I had gone hiking alone in the mountains, and I was ready to climb further up a steep ledge when I heard what sounded like the flutter of gigantic wings. I looked around, and no one was there; then I sensed the Lord's Presence and the Holy Spirit strongly warning me not to take another step. I withdrew my foot and re-traced my steps back off that mountain. Had I taken that step, I am convinced I would have fallen off that ledge. The Bible says of the angels in Hebrews 1:14, *"Are they not all ministering spirits sent forth to minister for those who will inherit salvation?"*

Pastor Sees Glory Cloud

In 1994, during my trip to Malaysia, a revival broke out, and angels were heard singing in the Anglican Church in Kuching, East Malaysia. They were singing, "Get ready, get ready, for Jesus is coming soon." During these particular meetings, some of the precious Chinese people were caught up in the glory, the meetings lasting until 2:30 A.M. Many who were under a heavy anointing could not get up, for they were stuck on the floor; others were laughing uncontrollably with holy laughter. Twice the *rushing mighty wind* swept through the church building. Once the pastor saw the glory like a cloudy mist on the platform, and some would fall out of their seats when I was preaching.

During the altar call, one usher was standing ready to help when the power of God hit him, and down he went. Another man tried to help someone off the floor, and when he touched the one under the glory, he literally flew through the air! Moreover, around the altar area, there were "holy rollers," mostly the young people. I have heard about "holy rollers" from the 1906 Azusa

Street revival that birthed the Pentecostal movement here in the United States, but I was astounded to see it firsthand in a church in Kuala Lumpur.

PROPHETIC WORD FOR MALAYSIA

A young 14-year-old prophet named Alton gave the following prophecy in his church in Alor Setar (pronounced aloe star), which is in the northern part of Malaysia near the Thailand border. He said, "Revival has come, the great awakening has begun in the North Star…do not seek my power but seek My presence, for when you have My presence, you will have My power." When the prophecy came forth, Pastor Clarine lifted the Malaysian flag and had the congregation stand and point their Bibles toward the flag; then they all sang the national anthem, declaring that Malaysia shall be a Christian nation. (Malaysia is a Muslim nation.) On that *same* night in Kuala Lumpur, which is on the southern part of Malaysia, a prophetic word came forth that Malaysia would become a Christian nation. If God spoke it, it will happen. What a glorious outpouring in both cities on the same night!

WHAT HAPPENS IN THE GLORY?

When the God of the universe touches you in a meeting or in your "prayer closet," you can have a terrible sense of your own weakness. Just as we saw with the outpouring in Malaysia, when He comes in power, all you can do is stand back and let God do His thing. This is what happened to Habakkuk when God responded to his cry for revival: *"When I heard, my body trembled; my lips quivered at the voice…"* (Hab. 3:16). Isaiah said that when God comes down in His splendor and glory, the mountains shake…and so do we. He said in Isaiah 64:2, *"As fire burns brushwood, as fire causes water to boil….*" I believe that is what happens when ministers are on fire while bringing the Word. They begin to perspire profusely. The fire upon their head causes the "wells of salvation" inside of them to boil over!

I recall so vividly my trip to Scotland, when I was helping a pastor friend of mine establish a small church in the outskirts of Glasgow; as I stood up to preach, the fire of God came on me, and I started to burn, and then perspiration flowed down my face. I cried out, "This is either the fire of God, or this is a menopausal hot flash!" The moving of the Lord's Presence in that meeting proved it was the fire of God.

Luke the physician recounts to us in the Book of Acts, chapter 2, the historical facts that occurred on the Day of Pentecost (which was 50 days after Jesus ascended to Heaven in bodily form after His resurrection from the dead). Luke writes,

> *When the Day of Pentecost had fully come…suddenly there came a sound from heaven, as of a rushing mighty wind…then there appeared to them divided tongues, as of fire, and one sat upon each of them. And they were all filled with the Holy Spirit and began to speak with other tongues as the Spirit gave them utterance…when this sound occurred, the multitude came together, and were confused…" we hear them speaking in our own tongues the wonderful works of God"…"Whatever could this mean?" Others mocking said, "They are full of new wine"* (Acts 2:1-13).

God knows how to attract people to a revival meeting. He uses signs and wonders, miracles and the glory to bring the people together so He can touch them, change them, and help them. Wind and fire are the visible manifestation of God's presence. In the Old

Testament, God initially appeared to Moses in a burning bush that was not consumed, and in many other places in Scripture, the Lord used fire to reveal His presence. In early 1993, a flaming evangelist from South Africa came to our city in Alaska.

During the height of the revival, a local minister came to the meeting with an attitude of "bless me if you can!" For some reason, I watched him when the altar call went forth. He just sat there with his arms folded tightly across his chest when all of a sudden a fireball (I did not see it, but I sure saw the results of it) from Heaven hit this man. His startled look of fear in his face told it all. His arms and legs shot straight out as he was pushed five rows back, the chairs piling up behind him! When I witnessed that, I thought, *Hit him again, Lord, hit him again!* Then I saw another fireball hit another man in the audience. After going under the power of God, he cried out as if he was burning. The people stared at him in fear, not wanting to move. The evangelist said that if the fire of God slammed you, you would be yelling out too!

WIND OF GOD BLOWS DOORS OPEN

During one of our winter Alaskan conferences, a minister friend of mine from Indiana was teaching the Word when he called for those who wanted a touch from the Lord to come forward. His ministry style at times can be quiet, which is good when you are prophesying over people. As he was ministering, I noticed one young man touched by the Lord lying on the cold floor. It got too quiet for me, so I got up and said to my friend Georgia, "I can't stand it when it gets too quiet; I pray the fire of God falls in this place!" Just as soon as those words got out of my mouth, the wind of God hit the two bolted doors and blew them open! The cold frigid January weather had forced the thermostats to work at its peak, and yet the building was still cold especially the wooden floors. When the wind blew open the doors, the young man on the floor heard the wind coming and thought he would really be freezing, but he testified later that the wind that blew from outside was warm! It was the wind of God or God's Presence that came into the meeting.

On another occasion, I was teaching in a small Bible school just outside of Spokane, Washington. The meetings always had anointed music, with spontaneous praise breaking forth, and then a time of deep worship to Jesus. At this one school, during the concluding service, I sang two songs before I was to bring the Word. I started to pray, "Father, in the name of Jesus, let the wind of God blow in this place and let the fire fall..." I had not even finished my prayer when the fire of God fell in that place. A pastor from Scotland fell almost violently to the floor; another minister went sliding off her chair, and several on the second row went sliding off their seats. It was as if someone put a match to gasoline—kaboom!

During the end of that meeting, the Lord told us to continue to prepare for what is coming, for it will be *more* than what we bargained for! I cannot imagine how the fire and glory could get greater, but I do not think we have seen anything yet. First Corinthians 4:20 says, *"For the kingdom of God is not in word but in power."*

THE GLORY WITHIN

Several years ago, I attended a seminar held in a church in Texas, and one of my classes was on angelic activation, according to Psalm 103:20: *"Bless the Lord, you His angels, who excel in strength, who do His word, heeding the voice of His word.*" At the conclusion of our workshop, our teacher, wanting to teach us how to discern the spirit realm, asked us to walk around the periphery of the sanctuary and pray in the spirit, letting him know if we could spiritually discern any angelic beings. I was a little skeptical but obedient. Most of the students were near the pulpit area, so I walked toward the back of the church.

While I was praying in tongues, one of the women called out, "Flo, come over here. I sense angels in this area." My traveling companion Brenda and I slowly walked toward the front. As we approached the middle aisle Brenda let out a groan, doubled over (obviously overcome by the Lord), and then started to worship the Lord. I moved cautiously toward her, and then suddenly the atmosphere changed, and I could sense the mighty presence of the Lord and His angels. The glory came upon my eyes, and I could feel a power emanating through them! I squinted and saw our teacher look at me with a startled look; then he almost flipped over and looked wide-eyed at me a second time. I could barely stand upright—the glory of the Lord was so strong on me. His presence remained on me all that day, even when we went to a restaurant for dinner.

After the class was over and I had gone back home to Washington state, I wrote to my instructor and asked him what he had seen when he almost fell backward. He sent me an e-mail and said,

> I will try and answer your question about what I saw during the angelic activation class. As I looked in the direction where you were standing, a brightness shown from your face, which was the glory of the Lord. It was so bright that I had to cover my face. There were obviously angels around you, but this glory seemed to be

emanating from within you. A biblical example that comes to mind was when Jesus was on the mount and transfigured before them (Matthew 17). The glory of the Lord was literally shining forth from your face. It was incredible.

As a safeguard, I usually call my spiritual mother-in-the Lord, Mother Jenkins to get her thoughts on any unusual spiritual experience I have had. After this experience, I called her and began to share with her what happened at the angel class; when I got to the part about the glory, she interrupted me and finished my sentence, saying, "And he had to cover his face because the glory was shining forth from you."

I responded in total surprise, "Yes, Mother. But how did you know?"

She said, "I saw it happen!" (Mother is a prophet; she sees and hears in the spirit.)

Since that early morning encounter many years ago, every time the glory comes, it hits my eyes first; they are "slain in the spirit," and all I can do is peer through. I do not understand why that happens; it just does. There are times when the glory is so heavy on me that I can hardly see or stand upright. These are days when the glory will increase in waves of splendor.

THE GLORY INCREASES

Many hungering for more of the Lord will be enraptured in His presence for hours, some for days. I have noticed that the more critical, skeptical, or distant from the Lord we are, the less plausible we find the supernatural to be. The Holy Spirit told me many years ago that the things that happened in the Bible would happen in our day.

Some are afraid to enter into this move of God because of the excesses they have witnessed. It is wise to be cautious and to not enter in until you are convinced it is of the Lord. However, there is a big difference between revelry, silliness, or foolishness and the joy of the Lord. The closer you are to the Lord, the quicker you will be able to discern between the profane, the counterfeit, and the holy; you will not miss what He has for you.

I stand in the company of all saints who desire to see more of God's glory. Habakkuk was also one who cried out to the Lord to see His glory, and when he did, this young prophet probably saw the greatest demonstration of God's glory any man has ever seen. He cried out,

> *O Lord, I have heard Your speech and was afraid;*
> *O Lord, revive Your work in the midst of the years!*
> *In the midst of the years, make it known;*
> *In wrath, remember mercy.*
> *God came...*
> *His glory covered the heavens...*
> *His brightness was like the light;*
> *He had rays flashing from His hand,*
> *And there His power was hidden.*
> (Habakkuk 3:1-4)

"God came!" When God comes...that *is* revival.

All over the world, the knowledge of the glory is coming through the saints in great signs, wonders, and miracles. I have been expecting the unprecedented glory to fall. My heart has longed for a new move of God in the earth. In 1992, the Holy Spirit spoke this prophetic word through me: "Ask largely of Me, saith the Lord, for this is the day of My power and the fulfillment of all that has been spoken by the prophet Joel. It is the day of the outpouring upon all flesh, for all shall see My glory. I will show up in the marketplaces; I will show up in the temples made with hands; I will show up in *the* temple [your spirit] made by My hands. Moreover, as you come into My presence, I will hear before you call; and I will answer before you ask; and I will heal before you cry out, for this is *the* day you longed for. This is the day of My glory. This is the day of My timing, saith the Lord, for the set time has now come!" Hallelujah!

It is the day when *Jesus* will manifest Himself through every believer. In America, we are preparing for that day, for the third awakening, and it will come with unprecedented power. (Perhaps, as you are reading this chapter, it has already begun!) Something big is on the horizon, and we are on the very threshold of it. Romans 8:18 says it best, *"For I consider that the sufferings of this present time (this present life) are not worth being compared with the glory that is about to be revealed to us and in us and for us and conferred on us"* (AMP).

ENDNOTES

1. James Strong, *The New Strong's Expanded Exhaustive Concordance of the Bible* (Nashville, TN: Thomas Nelson, 2001); "Hebrew Dictionary," *kabowd*, number 3519; "Greek Dictionary," *doxa*, number 1391.

2. Strong, "Greek Dictionary," *baros*, meaning "weight, load, abundance," number 922.

3. Strong, "Hebrew Dictionary," *achowr*, number 268.

Chapter 5

GREAT FAITH COMES FROM
KNOWING A GREAT GOD

Bursting through the doorway of the humble Mexican house, a strange woman came in crying, "I can see, I can see!"

"What happened?" Sister Henysel asked her in Spanish. The woman said that when she heard a woman singing, the power of God came upon her, and her blind eye opened!

When I heard this woman's testimony of a healing that she had neither asked for nor expected, I suddenly thought back to a word my good friend Pastor Sam from Oklahoma gave me shortly before I left for Mexico. As we were finishing our conversation about my upcoming trip, he said to me with a clipped military voice, as only he can modulate, "Flo, you are being *sent* as you have never been *sent!*"

I met Brother and Sister Henysel, my traveling companions, at the border town of Nogales, Arizona, and we drove down to

Bacabachi, Sonora, Mexico, to meet some pastor friends of the Henysels and to do a couple of days of meetings in the area. When we arrived at the church, I first noticed the perfectly-spaced, white streamers on the church fascia blowing in the warm wind and the freshly swept entryway. How clean, I thought. It seems the Holy Spirit restores everything to its pristine beauty when the spirit of revival comes—this church was no exception.

As I was admiring the neatness of the church grounds, I saw a tanned, medium-built man coming toward us. As I stared at him, I heard the Holy Spirit say to me, "He is an apostle." Sister Henysel said, "Sister Flo, this is Brother Yocopicio, pastor of this church. He is the man I told you about." While we were exchanging pleasantries, a tall, lean, dark-haired woman in a simple printed dress walked toward us, carrying in her gait the glory of God with regal dignity. I again heard the voice of the Lord, and He said, "She is a prophetess." Brother Yocopicio introduced her as his mother. She had piercing dark eyes, and as she was looking deep into my eyes, she exclaimed, "The Lord told me a *sent* one was coming to us from Alaska!" (At that time, I was living in the state where I was born—Alaska.) I stood there speechless, thinking about what Pastor Sam said when Pastor Yocopicio broke the silence, asking us if we would like to go to a home where a brother was very sick of a great fever and pray for his healing. We all agreed and followed them to a small, humble home.

When we walked through the door, it took a few moments for our eyes to adjust from the bright sunlight to the darkness in the room. Over in the corner of the living room, pushed up against the wall, was a small cot with a man laying on it. He had on a cap and was wrapped up tightly in a patchwork quilt, shivering.

Brother Yocopicio said, "This is the man who is sick." Sister Henysel came over to me and asked me to sing one of my songs before we prayed. (I thought, *Sing here? Right now?*)

I told her that my soundtracks were in the vehicle and that I did not have a cassette player (thinking I would not have to sing) when Brother Yocopicio said, "We have one!"

I quickly ran out to the station wagon and picked "Rise and Be Healed" to sing. I put the track in the cassette player, and a young man put it on his shoulder. With my "sound system" in place, I closed my eyes and began to sing, strongly feeling the words of the song, "...so rise and be healed in the Name of Jesus, just let faith arise in your soul..."

Just as I finished singing, this woman came bursting through the door and cried out, "I can see! I can see!" When she got her emotions under control, she told us that she was in the next house when she heard a woman singing; while she listened, she felt the power of God come upon her, and her blind eye opened. When she finished giving her testimony, we all rejoiced for what Jesus had done for her.

Then we began to pray for the sick man. Sister Hensyel directed me to do the praying. I bent over to touch the man, and when I laid my hands on him, I felt his body shivering uncontrollably although it was well over 90 degrees outside. *A devil has put a terrible fever on him, I thought.* As I began to pray, I sensed a power in the room that left *me* shaking. I looked at Sister Henysel and whispered, "*What* is *this* power I am sensing in this room?"

She said, "Oh, this is the house the Yocopicio family laid on their faces in for a year (when they got kicked out of their denomination) after they were baptized in the Holy Spirit. They cried out to the Lord to teach them about *this* Holy Spirit and His power."

That was the power I was feeling, and it was powerful. We prayed for the young man, and then left for the place where we were to stay for the next couple of days of meetings.

After we finished our ministry, Pastor Yocopicio asked me to teach him about the Holy Spirit and God's power. I thought to myself, *You want me to teach you? You should teach me.* Through our preaching and in our simple way, we taught them a little of what we knew of the great third person of the Trinity—the Holy Spirit.

This incident reminded me of what my friend Reverend Lynda told me many years ago: "Flo, if I had it all, I would not need you. I do not have it all; therefore, I need you." That is humility.

For decades, the United States has been sending missionaries to the nations of the world. What we have sown, we are now reaping as missionaries from other countries are coming to us to preach the Word. As we cross-pollinate the Gospel, we learn from one another. When our ministry was finished in Mexico, we traveled back to the United States, grateful to the Lord for the honor of meeting such godly saints. We said our goodbyes, promising to return in the Lord's timing.

CHOSEN AND UNIQUELY ANOINTED

And He [Jesus] went up on the mountain and called to Him those He Himself wanted. And they came to Him. Then He appointed twelve, that they might be with Him and that He might send them out to preach, and to have power to heal sicknesses and to cast out demons (Mark 3:13-15).

Perhaps when you read these verses, you are tempted to compare yourself with these men who were chosen by Jesus and anointed with power and say, "I am not like the apostles—or the ministers in Mexico who lay on their faces for a year." That is true, but the Lord wants to flow through all faith-filled believers. He has a plan for the believers in Mexico, and He has a plan for you. First Corinthians 12:7 states, "*But the manifestation of the Spirit is given to each one for the profit of all….*"

Just as each fingerprint is different, so are we in our personalities, in our callings, and in the precious anointing flowing through each one of us. Each person is unique, an original; there is no one quite like you in the earth—so it is with the work of the ministry. As *you* yield to the Holy Spirit, there will be an uncommon and extraordinary expression of His Kingdom flowing through you. Romans 12:4-6 tells us,

For as we have many members in one body, but all the members do not have the same function, so we, being many, are one body in Christ, and individually members of one another. Having then gifts differing according to the grace that is given to us, let us use them.

The Holy Spirit's gifts, or *spirituals*, are divine abilities to meet every human need. All nine gifts are *in* the Person of the Holy Spirit, and if you are a born-again believer in Jesus Christ, then the *spirituals* can flow through you (because the Holy Spirit resides in you). The Holy Spirit's delivery of the gifts is as *He* wills, but He will need you to cooperate with Him. By your faith, you release those gifts, but you must first build yourself up in your most holy faith (see Jude 1:20).

> One of the ways is to build up your faith is by reading the Word of God, especially the Gospels of Matthew, Mark, Luke, and John. As you read and reread the accounts of the miracles of Jesus, you will begin to see yourself doing the very works of Christ. At first, you will marvel at the miracles of Christ; then, as you reread the Gospels, the revelation that Christ lives in you will dawn upon you, and you will begin to see yourself flowing with the Holy Spirit and doing these same works. All this takes faith.

GOING FROM "FAITH TO FAITH"

There are two kinds of faith. The fruit of the Spirit (*faith*) as listed in Galatians 5:22 and the sign gift (*gift of faith*) in First Corinthians 12:9. There are also two qualities of faith: substance and evidence. Hebrews 11:1 says, "*Now faith is the substance [the essence or reality] of things hoped for, the evidence [the proof] of things not seen*" (AMP).

Faith and hope are two different powers. Someone once said that you could hope for a million and die penniless. Isaiah 7:9 says, "*If you will not believe, surely you shall not be established.*" If your faith is locked on to God's Word and His promises, you will be strong, and the enemy of your soul will not be able to dissuade you from your course of action. Hebrews 6:11-12 exhorts us to "*show the same diligence to the full assurance of hope until the end, that you do not become sluggish, but imitate those who through faith and patience inherit the promises."*

To develop your faith, you must start by taking small steps of obedience as the Holy Spirit nudges you. (I learned these principles from the Holy Spirit, as well as from Lester Sumrall and other giants of the faith that have finished their course.) As you obey every instruction, the Holy Spirit will take you into higher degrees of faith until your joy is full. The following Scriptures have much to say about the disciples' faith. As you read them, you will see how the Lord took them step-by-step into an exciting walk with Him. He wants to take you on the same path.

First, every disciple (including you) is given a *"...measure of faith"* (Rom. 12:3). That measure does not have to remain at the same level. It is up to you. Every time you exercise your faith, you will grow in confidence. Romans 1:17 tells us, *"For in it the righteousness of God is revealed from faith to faith; as it is written, the just shall live by faith."* In the first level, we have what I call *"measuring faith."* We received that measure when we were first born-again.

If we are to go from "faith to faith," then this "measuring faith" is the doorway by which we will access those greater levels of faith. Romans 4:19 tells us that Abraham, *"not being weak in faith,"* did not allow the state of his body to cause him to waver in faith. One sign, therefore, of weak faith is the ease with which our circumstances can cause us to move into unbelief. We overcome weak faith by not looking at the circumstances that are screaming at us, but by believing that what God said He would do, He *will* do.

In this portion of Scripture, it says about Abraham, *"He did not waver at the promise of God through unbelief, but was strengthened in faith, giving glory to God, and being fully convinced that what He had promised He was also able to perform*" (Rom. 4:20-21). Abraham refused to look at the deadness of Sarah's womb and his inability to reproduce. What you focus on will become big in your eyes. For instance, if you continually look at your symptoms, you will not get well. If you look at your poverty instead of looking at the provisions promised in the Word of God, you will continue to walk in lack. As you focus upon, reading and recounting, the promises out loud (so your own ears and spirit hear the Word), your faith will begin to grow in substance, and you will soon see the evidence of what you have been believing for.

In the account in Matthew 8:23-27, Jesus and His disciples encountered a great storm on the sea of Galilee, but Jesus was so at rest in His Father's plan for His life that He was asleep in the stern of the boat as it was tossed on the sea. The disciples were in fear and dread, for they were about to capsize and drown (and when fishermen get fearful, you *know* it is a horrific storm with gale forces that *really* could overturn the boat!).

They finally went to Jesus, shaking Him awake, and cried out, "*Lord, save us! We are perishing!*" Jesus crawled out of the bow of the boat, stood up, and said to them, "*Why are you fearful, O you of **little faith**?*" (*Little faith, Jesus? The boat is about to roll over, and you want to talk to us about "little faith"?*) With all authority, Jesus rebuked the winds and waves, and a great, eerie calm settled upon the sea; the disciples looked at each other in astonishment and said, "*Who can this be, that even the winds and the sea obey Him?*"

When you are compliant with the Holy Spirit's instruction, your "*faith grows exceedingly,*" as the Word reveals to us in Second Thessalonians 1:3. Do you see the advancement of your faith? It is beginning to grow—exceedingly. Years ago, before I would stand behind a pulpit to preach or teach the Word, I used to battle with timidity until I read Proverbs 28:1 *"The wicked flee when no man pursueth: but the righteous are bold as a lion."* I would quote that Word over and over until one day, I stood up to preach, and to my amazement, that spirit of fear was gone. As that portion of Scripture went into my spirit, my faith continued to grow exceedingly until there was more room for the fear of man because it was replaced by the boldness of Jesus.

We have gone from *measuring faith to weak in faith to little faith* and have now progressed to a *faith that grows exceedingly.* You are no longer wavering in the sin of unbelief. Romans 4:20 reveals to us that Abraham refused to look at his own body—now 100 years old—and Sarah's barren womb—now well past menopause. It was impossible for her to bear a child, but with God, all things are possible! Abraham believed God's Word, and God honored his faith by giving them their promised child—Isaac. (As we said in a previous chapter, *Isaac* means "laughter," so God got the last laugh. Ha!)

The next degree of faith is *"great faith."* Matthew 8:5-13 tells us of the story of the centurion's servant who was healed by Jesus. This centurion came to Jesus, pleading for his paralyzed servant who was dreadfully tormented by demons. Jesus told him that He would come to his house and heal him, but the centurion protested, *"Lord, I am not worthy that You should come under my roof. But only speak a word, and my servant will be healed…."* Jesus marveled at this man's humility and mature faith and said, *"Assuredly, I say to you, I have not found such **great faith**…."*

 Great faith comes from being humble. Jesus said to the centurion, *Go your way; and as you have believed, so let it be done for you. And his servant was healed that same hour."*

A miracle is instantaneous; a healing can sometimes take longer. If the Lord is healing you, do not look at the symptoms which may be deceptive, but remain in faith, and you will see the total manifestation of your healing. Healings do take longer sometimes; they are not always instantaneous.

James 2:5 says, "*Has God not chosen the poor of this world to be **rich in faith**....*" Many times, I have wondered why American evangelists who go to other countries see creative miracles, the dead raised, and the multitudes healed of every malady. Then they come home with a glowing report, putting the photos on their websites, but when they are invited to meetings here in the U.S., they do not see any miracles. As I pondered that, I heard in my spirit that the reason Americans see such results in other nations is because they come under that nation's anointing and faith. However, here in our nation, rather than faith for the lost and dying, some have faith primarily for prosperity, material wealth, our own jets, Rolex watches, and seven-bedroom mansions; our preaching and conferences reflect such a mindset. Our emphasis is misplaced.

It is great to have stuff, but we need to grow in faith like the poor who are "*rich in faith*" for healings, resurrections, and creative miracles. I am not against prosperity in any area of my life, but any truth taken to an extreme becomes perverted or unbalanced at best. We need to get back to what really matters—to the faith of our fathers. As we have witnessed the miracles in the nations, it has caused us to become hungry to see such a move in America, but it will come with a price. While *Pentecost* literally means "50th," the word can also be a visual reminder of what a demonstration of biblical power will *cost* us. To see this kind of move of

God, you must be willing to pay the same price as the leaders of the Chinese underground church, or the Russian underground church, or the church in Africa. You will pay with your life.

True faith requires dying to self.

It would be good to re-read Hebrews 11:13,39-40, *"These all died in faith...And all these, having obtained a good testimony through faith, did not receive the promise, God having provided something better for us, that they should not be made perfect [or complete] apart from us,"* or Psalm 145:4, *"One generation shall praise Thy works to another, and shall declare Thy mighty acts"* (KJV).

In the past seven years, a deep work has been done in the hearts of the crossover generation, those who love Jesus with all their hearts. The godly generation alive today is the one that will supersede the first generation of believers in the Book of Acts because there is a quality of faith that has fully matured. Jude 1:3 says,

> *"Beloved, my whole concern was to write to you in regard to our common salvation. [But] I found it necessary and was impelled to write you and urgently appeal to and exhort [you] to contend for the faith which was once for all handed down to the saints [the faith which is that sum of Christian belief which was delivered verbally to the holy people of God]"* (AMP).

In Church history, after what was known as the Dark Ages, each succeeding generation thereafter received a truth that was lost to the Church. Thus, the present generation is walking in more truth than any preceding generation. Truth is power. This generation is rising up in the faith and power that was once delivered to the early disciples.

In 1995, a young convert, while listening to my preaching, said the Lord inspired her to write the following poem. I believe it represents the battle cry of this generation, a generation that is bold and fearless, and that walks in uncompromising faith.

We are the generation of the Lord.
We're arising for battle at His command,
He is sounding the trumpet
To take back the land.
City by city we're claiming our right,
To worship our Lord on every night;

In God we trust, we are taking a stand,
We're putting our nation back in His Hand!

Let us now go to the next level of Abraham's faith found in James 2:21-22, *"Was not Abraham our father justified by works when he offered Isaac his son on the altar? Do you see that faith was working together with his works, and by works **faith was made perfect** [mature or complete]?"* Faith produces works; and works makes faith perfect or mature.

One of the early Pentecostal pioneers said, "Faith is an act!" A minister friend of mine once said, "I believe in works by salvation, not salvation by works." Faith works.

The highest degree of faith may be found in the life and ministry of Stephen, the Church's first martyr. Stephen was a man of tested character, filled with and controlled by the Holy Spirit, who flowed through him in signs, wonders, and miracles. Acts 6:5 says, *"And they chose Stephen, a man **full of faith** and the Holy Spirit…."*

FAITH ACTS

In the early fall of 1991, the Holy Spirit led me on my second 40-day fast without telling me what the fast was for; in total obedience, I abstained from food, drinking only water. On the morning of the 40th day, I was awakened by the sound of my own agonizing cry. I felt a sharp, stabbing pain in my chest, and the Holy Spirit said, "Call your doctor and make an appointment." After meeting with my Christian doctor, I was directed to go immediately to the lab for chest x-rays, which revealed a tumor. My doctor admitted me to the hospital, and I underwent a lumpectomy. While waiting for the test results, I got up three times in the middle of the night and asked the Lord, "Is this cancer? What will be the outcome?" Each time He responded, "Yes, this is cancer, but *within* three months you will be just fine."

With that inside information, and a specific promise from the Lord, I was poised for the battle.

My husband wanted me to undergo radiation and chemotherapy, and I agreed to his request. I underwent six weeks of radiation and chemotherapy by mouth and by injection. As the weeks went by, the doctors told me I would get weaker and weaker, but amazingly, I got stronger and stronger. Toward the end of my treatments, my hair started falling out by the handfuls until you could see my scalp. Throughout this ordeal, I think that was the only thing that really bothered me!

Before I was diagnosed with this "aggressive cancer," I had scheduled my first "Mighty Warriors Conference," slated for early spring, 1991, in Midwest City, Oklahoma, with special speaker Rodney Howard-Browne. Two weeks before the radiation and chemo treatments were finished, I received a call from my good minister friend Sheila, a woman of God of great faith. I told her I was still planning to have my Oklahoma conference regardless of what the doctors advised. One week later, she arrived with her intercessor and checked into a hotel near the Seattle airport. They began to pray with diligence for me, claiming Scriptures regarding my hair loss and my health. On my last day of treatment, the doctor's staff came to me and told me they had miscalculated the number of radiation treatments. Rather than this being my last day (which was Thursday), I needed three more sessions.

I was dismayed at the news but was determined to go to my scheduled conference, so I submitted to all three treatments being given to me in one day! (That was Friday.) Having three radiation treatments in one day should have totally wiped me out physically, but God was in control of my life. When the technician finished the last dose of radiation, I did not wait for the bed to be lowered but jumped off it before the tech could stop me. He looked a little perturbed, reaching out with a helping hand to catch this "witless" woman. When I did not fall, he breathed a sigh of relief and said with a smile on his face, "I hope I *never* see you again Mrs. Ellers." With that, I grinned back at him, doubled up my fist, raised it in the air, and yelled, "HALLELUJAH!" as I walked down the hall and out of that hospital. I am sure that tech thought I was crazy!

The next morning, I looked in the mirror, and all of my hair had grown back supernaturally! *"With God all things are possible."* Come on, Jesus!

Two days later, I was on my plane heading for Oklahoma. The "Mighty Warriors Conference" started on Monday. For four glorious days, 300 key Native American leaders had a Holy Spirit explosion of signs, wonders, and miracles—and drank the "new wine" (Acts 2:15, *"these are not drunken as ye suppose"*). The fire of

God fell upon the participants, and the liberty of the Holy Spirit was expressed in jubilant whooping, shouting, and dancing. I too danced and twirled and danced some more during those four days as the Spirit filled my temple with joy unspeakable and full of glory! Ha! And *they* said I would get weaker and weaker!

On the fourth night, Brother Rodney was powerfully preaching from the Book of Acts when the atmosphere, charged with the healing Presence of Jesus, came upon me as I was sitting on the front row. Brother Rodney said repeatedly from Acts 19:20, "*So mightily grew the Word of God and prevailed. So mightily grew the Word of God and prevailed. So mightily grew the Word of God and prevailed,*" when suddenly the anointing hit me! I was starting to slide off my seat, and I could not speak. I thought, *Not **now** Lord, not when Brother Rodney is preaching!* But the Lord did not respond to my plea. Suddenly, what felt like a hand came over my mouth and started to smother me. I started to panic because I could not breathe. I was trying desperately to get air when my arms fell at my side with my left arm dangling. A man behind me panicked, grabbed my hand, and tried to console me but Brother Rodney said in a low commanding voice, "Leave her alone, she will be alright." I thought, *Yeah, that's easy for **you** to say…you are not the one being smothered!* Just as quickly as the first hand came upon me, I felt the hand of the Lord press down over my face; I sensed His powerful hand ripping away the hand that was smothering me, peeling back its fingers, and I was free! I inhaled deeply and slowly sat erect, regaining my composure and dignity. After the meeting, three brothers came to me, and one prophet said, "I have to tell you what I saw in the spirit, Sister Flo. When you went down, I saw the hand of the Lord come upon you and rip the spirit of death off of you!"

When I got home, I gave my testimony to my husband Mike, and then squealed, "Mike, it was exactly *two days* short of three months when Jesus healed me at the conference. Remember, what the Lord said to me when I discovered I had cancer. He said, 'Yes, it is cancer, but *within* three months you will be just fine.'" Oh, the Lord is never late and never early—always just on time.

Since that day, I have stood on Nahum 1:7a,9b, "*The Lord is good, a stronghold in the day of trouble; and He knows those who trust in Him....Affliction will not rise up a second time.*" The cancer has never returned.

"It is Well"

Do you remember the story in Second Kings 4:8-37 when Elisha raised the Shunammite's son from the dead? Elisha used to pass by this Shunammite's home and have a meal with her and her husband. One day, this woman asked her husband if they could make an "upper room" for the man of God to stay in when he was passing through their city, and her husband agreed.

This woman made room for the anointing.

One day, Elisha (a type of Christ) said to his servant Gehazi (a type of the Holy Spirit), go find out what she needs or wants. She has been so kind; I want to bless her. She, being a humble woman, would not articulate her desire, so Gehazi interjected and told Elisha that she did not have a son. Elisha said, "*Call her'...she stood in the doorway. Then he said, 'About this time next year you shall embrace a son.' And she said, 'No, my lord. Man of God, do not lie to your maidservant.'*" In other words, she was implying that he did not have the power to give her this son because her husband was very old, and her time was past.

> Nevertheless, it is never too late for God. Your time has not passed. You can still give birth. You can give birth to your child or to a ministry; you can conceive your vision and bring it forth in the power of the Lord. It is not too late. Second Kings 4:17 declares that *"the woman conceived and bore a son when the appointed time had come...."* What is impossible with man is possible with God.

Sometime later, when the child had grown, he went out to the field where his father and the reapers were, and because of the heat of the day, he became deathly ill. The father had him taken to his mother, but the boy soon died of heatstroke. When the woman looked at her dead son, she must have thought, *The man who gave him to me when it was impossible is the same man who will give him life again.* She laid her son on the bed in the upper room that she had prepared for the man of God. She had her servants get her donkey ready, and she said, *"I will run to the man of God...and come back."*

She told her servants to drive on and to not be concerned with her well-being. She found the man on Mount Carmel; when he saw her in the distance, riding as fast as she could, he sent his servant Gehazi to ask her, *"'Is it well with you? Is it well with your husband? Is it well with the child?' And she answered, 'It is well.'"* Here her son was dead, but being a woman of faith, she refused to look at her dead son and responded to Gehazi, *"It is well."* At the end of the story, Elisha followed her back to the upper room where the dead child was laid; he shut the door and laid on the child twice until the Shunammite's son came back to life.

When the child sneezed seven times (the number of completion), every obstruction was gone, and life had returned, all because the Shunammite stood in faith and made room for the anointing.

Elisha called for the woman and said, *"Pick up your son'...so she picked up her son and went out."* It may be that your ministry looks dead, but if you will take it back to the Man of God, that which appears dead will receive life once again. If you have left your ministry, it is time to pick it back up. For the same fire that fell in the upper room on the Day of Pentecost came into that upper room where the dead child was raised back to life. In this story, the mother who conceived was also the one who had faith for a resurrection.

It is never too late for God to act.

Elisha, the man of God, told the woman, *"About this time next year you shall embrace a son."* Whatever the Lord has said to you, it is through *"faith and patience* [that you will] *inherit the promises"* (Heb. 6:12). However, you have to stand on the personal word the Lord gives to you through your time of prayer. It is called a *rhema word*, or the *now word* of God, for your particular situation.

Once you know that this is *your* promise from God, never let it go. Let your faith get a hold of God's word, and *with* the Holy Spirit, stand firm, knowing that what He has said He is well able to perform—no matter how impossible it may seem to you or to others around you. Numbers 23:19 reminds us, *"God is not a man, that He should lie, nor a son of man, that He should repent. Has He said, and will He not do? Or has He spoken, and will He not make it good?"*

Chapter 6

THE POWER OF GOD
UPON YOU

We have learned that the purpose of the glory is to change us in every area of our lives, but more importantly, it is to set us apart for God's use. In Second Corinthians 4:7 we read, *"...we possess this precious treasure [the divine Light of the Gospel] in [frail, human] vessels of earth, that the grandeur and exceeding greatness of the power may be shown to be from God and not from ourselves"* (AMP). The glory of the Lord will come upon when you are in deep prayer or when you are worshipping Him. In those times, when you adore the Lord from the very depths of your heart, you may feel a strong hand that causes you to tremble, or you may feel the fire or a peace that flows over you like warm honey or a silence so holy that you just lay or sit quietly, saying nothing while reverencing Him.

These are precious moments never repeated, so stay in His *presence until* the glory lifts.

When I was first born again, in 1971, I attended a Women's Aglow retreat, and while we were quietly worshiping Jesus, a presence came upon me, a power I had never experienced before. It so frightened me that I started to gasp in fear, but the Holy Spirit reassured me that this was holy, and I did not need to fear. His presence came again and left me feeling loved and warm inside. Over the years, the glory of the Lord has come upon me in many different ways. Sometimes I am under the power of God in a trance; sometimes I sit quietly; sometimes I laugh; sometimes I just bask in His love, singing in tongues or admiring His handiwork in the heavens.

I have learned through the Word and by my own experiences that I usually cannot function when God's eternal weight of glory comes upon me as it did on the 120 priests in the Old Testament (see 2 Chron. 5:14). If that same glory comes upon me when I am preaching, it usually comes upon the audience too because the Lord just wants to touch His people. Every time His glory comes upon us, we will be changed more and more into His likeness.

Flowing in this power, I have observed that, in the glory, I usually cannot function; in the anointing, I do everything better. Having said that, I in no way want to imply that these are two different powers. Both the glory and the anointing *are* the Presence of God Almighty. The glory is usually for you, and the anointing is for ministry.

150

THE PURPOSE OF GOD'S POWER

The apostle John said about Jesus, *"For this purpose the Son of God was manifested, that He might destroy the works of the devil"* (1 John 3:8b). Jesus now lives in the life of every believer. And He still lives to destroy the works of the devil, but now He does it through us.

We know that satan has some miraculous power that is designed to steal, kill, and destroy, but Jesus said in Matthew 28:18, *"All authority* [all power] *has been given to Me in heaven and on earth."* Today, He exercises His authority over devils through His saints. Luke 10:19 tells us what Jesus is saying to the Church, *"Behold, I give unto* **you** *power* [exousia—delegated power] *to tread on serpents and scorpions and over all the power* [dunamis—miraculous power] *of the enemy: and nothing shall by any means hurt you"* (KJV). Jesus said that He has *"all power,"* so that means He has both *exousia* and *dunamis* over satan. We exercise or demonstrate that power and authority over the demonic realm.

We need this power or anointing of God if we are going to set people free. Isaiah 10:27b tells us what the purpose of the anointing is: *"...the yoke* [anything that binds] *will be destroyed because of the anointing...."* The anointing of God is simply God in your flesh doing what you cannot possibly do. Ephesians 3:20 says, *"Now to Him who is able to do exceedingly abundantly above all that we ask or think, according to the power* [dunamis] *that works in us."* He wants to use you to set others free.

One of the words for "power" in the New Testament is *dunamis*, from which we get the word *dynamite*. In Greek, it means an inherent power capable of reproducing itself like a dynamo. *Inherent* means "existing in someone or something as a natural and

151

inseparable quality."[1] The Lord of glory will manifest Himself through us: "...God willed to make known...the riches of the glory of this mystery among the Gentiles: which is Christ in you, the hope of glory" (Col. 1:27).

The anointing that God put upon Jesus was the presence and power of God manifested. The word *manifest* means to "make clear or evident"; in our context, it can mean to bring out of the spiritual world into the physical world.[2] Every time Jesus obeyed His Father, the anointing of God released power from the spiritual world into our world. That "power" was the Person of the Holy Spirit. Without His ability working through us, our work is unacceptable. It is "*Not by might, nor by power* [our might or our power] *but by My Spirit,' says the Lord of hosts*" (Zech. 4:6b). When God met with Abraham, He told him that a child would come from his own loins, but Abraham said to the Lord, "*O that Ishmael might live before you*" (Gen. 17:18). God said no. (Ishmael was Abraham's son born to him through Hagar, his wife Sarah's maid.) *Isaac*, the son of promise, is what God had in mind, not the son of Abraham's flesh. The works we plan and carry out from our own fleshly minds are unacceptable to the Lord. Only the works of the spirit—only what the Holy Spirit initiates—will He bless.

THE ANOINTING OF GOD

The anointing is synonymous with oil, and that oil can leak through any hole, even the smallest crack. In Ephesians 4:26-27, Paul wrote, "*'Be angry and do not sin': do not let the sun go down on your wrath, nor give place to the devil.*" To "give place" means to provide a window or an avenue for the devil to get through or work through.

The only way to keep the devil out is to stay filled with the Holy Spirit.

Paul then went on to admonish his readers in 5:17-18, "...*understand what the will of the Lord is...do not be drunk with wine...but be filled with the Spirit....*" That word *filled* is in the continual sense: "be being filled." In other words, you can have many "Pentecosts" and be filled again and again. You can ask the Lord to fill you right now. Say, "Lord, your Word says in Psalm 92:10 that You caused the psalmist's horn to be exalted like a wild ox, and You anointed him with fresh oil, so will You fill me right now with this fresh oil?" Now, thank Jesus for filling you with the Holy Spirit.

We have many ministers today who cannot relax after a meeting until they have their glass of wine or a cordial or a can of beer. Jesus said, "...*do not be drunk* [intoxicated] *with wine, but be filled* [to cram, satisfy, cover over, to imbue, to make replete] *with the Holy Spirit*" (Eph. 5:18). Be filled with the Holy Spirit before the meeting, during the meeting, and after the meeting.

It is possible to stay filled by praying in tongues. Never be satisfied with where you are right now. There is always more, much more.

My good friend Pastor Sam always said, "Jesus is always greater than your last experience of Him." I do not know about you, but I have had some encounters and experiences with the Lord that were almost glorious beyond words; nevertheless, He is telling us, *there is more, so much more...so press in by staying filled with the Holy Spirit.*

153

FIVE WISE VIRGINS

The five foolish virgins in Matthew 25:1-13 are a prophetic picture of the last days' Church. The passage says,

The Kingdom of heaven shall be likened to ten virgins who took their lamps and went out to meet the bridegroom [Jesus]. Five of them were wise, and five were foolish. Those who were foolish took their lamps ["Thy Word is a lamp unto my feet," the psalmist said] *and took no oil* [oil is symbolic of the power of the Holy Spirit] *with them, but the wise took oil in their vessels with their lamps. But while the bridegroom was delayed, they all slumbered and slept. And at midnight, a cry was heard: "Behold, the bridegroom* [Jesus] *is coming; go out to meet him!"*

A fool will not prepare himself or herself for the Lord's coming. Do you know that there are more Scriptures concerning Jesus' second coming than there are about His first coming? He is coming soon! Are you ready?

Matthew 25 goes on to say,

Then all the virgins arose and trimmed their lamps. And the foolish said to the wise, "Give us some of your oil, for our lamps are going out." But the wise answered, saying, "No, lest there should not be enough for us and you; but go rather to those who sell, and buy for yourselves." And while they went to buy, the bridegroom came, and those who were ready went in with him to the wedding; and the door was shut.

When Jesus comes, it will be too late to *get* ready—you have to *be* ready.

In Ephesians 5:15-18, Paul advised,

> *See then that you walk circumspectly, not as fools but as wise, redeeming the time, because the days are evil. There-fore, do not be unwise, but understand what the will of the Lord is...do not be drunk with wine, in which is dissipation* [or decadence and depravity], *but be filled* [continually filled] *with the Spirit....*

When you are filled with the presence and the power of the Holy Spirit, He will flow through you in ways you only dreamed about, bringing great glory and honor to Jesus. Proverbs 21:20 says, *"There is desirable treasure, and oil in the dwelling of the wise, but a foolish man squanders it."* The world needs what you have, so stay filled!

INCREASE OF THE ANOINTING

The anointing can increase upon your life; the anointing of God can be measured. Elisha had twice as much as Elijah. (See 2 Kings 2:9.) You are the one who sets the limit or boundary. John the Baptist spoke of Jesus in these terms: *"For since He whom God has sent speaks the words of God [proclaims God's own message] God does not give Him His Spirit sparingly or by measure, but boundless is the gift God makes of His Spirit"* (John 3:34 AMP).

There is no stopping off place with Jesus. The Bible declares that we can go from the *Spirit without measure* (see John 3:34) to the *baptismal measure* (see Matt. 3:11) to the *fullness of God* (see Eph. 3:19) to the *rivers of living waters* (see John 7:37-39), and fi-nally, to the *full anointing of the Spirit, endued with power from on high* (see Luke 24:49).[3]

YOU SHALL BE…

Acts 1:8 declares, *"But you shall receive power* [dunamis] *when the Holy Spirit comes upon you, and* **you shall be** *witnesses to Me in Jerusalem, and in all Judea and Samaria, and to the ends of the earth."*

"…you shall be…." Be what? Anything He needs you to be. All of who God is for us is wrapped up in His names; in this sense, *Jehovah* means, "I am becoming to you just what you need just when you need it; if you need salvation, I am your Savior; if you need healing; I am your Healer; if you need deliverance, I am your great Deliverer." Maybe you will be one who is called like Nehemiah, the apostolic leader who pursued the Israelites' spiritual and physical welfare. On the other hand, you may be like Mary Magdalene, who was the first evangelist to tell Jesus' disciples that He rose from the dead. (Mary Magdalene had seven devils cast out of her!) You shall be whatever He needs you to be. That is the divine exchange: He will be what you need (Jehovah-Rapha, Jehovah-Shalom, etc.), and you will be what He needs you to be for your generation.

"…witnesses to Me…." The word *witness* means "martyr." *Merriam-Webster's* says a martyr is someone who makes a great sacrifice for the sake of principle; a person who dies rather than renounces their faith.[4] Nevertheless, what Jesus is looking for is not a dead martyr but a live martyr, for He can do so much more with someone who is willing to live their faith in the face of persecution, suffering, and affliction.

Several years ago, I met a pastor who was a Communist before he gave his life totally to the Lord Jesus Christ. He told me a story of when he was living in the mountains of Mindanao. He accidentally shot his hand, and it became infected. He told the leader of his terrorist group that he had heard there was a Christian hospital at the bottom of the mountain where he could receive medical attention. His leader refused to allow him to go to "those Christians." He would rather that he suffer and die. He said that he did not mind dying for his cause, but he was not going to die for an accidental gunshot wound, so he slipped out during the night and made his way down the mountain to the hospital. They cleaned out the wound and ministered the love of Christ to him, and he gave his heart to Jesus. As I ministered to him, he said with resolve, "I was willing to die for the cause of Communism; now I am ready to die for Jesus." This young pastor's faith and commitment left a deep impression on me. After we left that island and went back home, we heard on the news that there was a bloodbath on that very mountain, and many of the pastors were beheaded. I do not know if he was one of them, but if he was, he had an abundant entrance into the Presence of the Lord in Heaven.

THE HOLY SPIRIT WILL COME UPON YOU

Every time the dunamis power comes upon you, there is an increase of the anointing in your life, and the impossible becomes possible! Mary, Jesus' earthly mother, asked the angel Gabriel, *"'How can this be, since I do not know a man?' And the angel answered and said to her, 'The Holy Spirit will come upon you and the power* [dunamis] *of the Highest will overshadow you...'"* (Luke 1:34-35). The impossible became possible when the Holy Spirit's anointing came upon her.

In Acts 10, Peter preached to Cornelius' household about Jesus, who was *"anointed...with the Holy Spirit and with power, who went about doing good and healing all who were oppressed by the devil, for God was with Him"* (Acts 10:38). The words *went about* mean that He "walked through" or "wandered around" the streets

157

and marketplaces to find those oppressed with devils so that He could heal them.[5]

My precious friend Jody told me about her Apache friends (whom she loves dearly) who love to shop at a certain chain store. Because they get such super bargains, they call it "Apache heaven." I too love to shop there, and since I am a Tlingit/Cherokee Indian, we can also call it "Tlingit heaven" or "Cherokee heaven." Now, if Jesus were on the earth today, He would love to walk around this "Apache heaven" looking for the oppressed. Because He lives in us, He may want to wander around through you in many marketplaces. Be open to this, and if you find any sick (and you will), ask them if you can pray for them.

Most hurting people will not turn down prayer to alleviate their pain. If you lay hands on them, and they are not healed, it is OK. You have nothing to lose and no reputation to protect, since they do not know you and probably will never see you again. Then again, they *just* may receive their healing. If they do, give all the praise to Jesus. All Jesus wants is for you to do your part—lay hands on them; and He will do His part—heal them.

How God anointed Jesus of Nazareth with the Holy Ghost and with power; who went about doing good, and healing all that were oppressed of the devil; for God was with him (Acts 10:38).

IS GOD WITH YOU?

You may not be a television evangelist or a pastor, but you can have your own ministry by wandering around the marketplaces or the malls healing the sick, casting out devils, and telling them about Jesus. The sick, the hurting, and the dying do not care how much education you have, how rich you are, or how good looking you are. All they care about is getting well. Paul the apostle said, *"...my speech and my preaching was not with enticing words of man's wisdom, but in demonstration of the Spirit and of power [dunamis]"* (1 Cor. 2:4). Like my friend has said, you cannot lay your pastoral credentials or your theological degree on the sick and say, "In the name of *this* degree rise and be healed!" No, a thousand times, no. It is in the Name, which is above every other name in Heaven and on earth, that people are truly healed. When you say, "In the name of Jesus, be healed," something happens. It is not some formula or an incantation; no, there is power behind the name of Jesus spoken in faith by a believer.

When you go anywhere the Holy Spirit leads you, tell them your story of how Jesus set you free, how Jesus healed your body, and how Jesus saved your soul. This is your calling; this is your ministry. The Bible says in a very pointed way in Second Corinthians 5 that, because we know *"the terror of the Lord, we persuade men.... And...God...hath reconciled us to Himself...and hath given to us the **ministry of reconciliation**"* (2 Cor. 5:10-11;18). We who have been reconciled to God have the great privilege and responsibility to tell others about Jesus Christ and His glorious salvation. That is what it means to have "the ministry of reconciliation"—so we all have a "ministry."

An Effective Ministry

To be a more effective witness and to have an effective ministry, you will need to read the Word, pray in tongues, and then obey whatever God tells you. Acts 5:32 says, *"And we are His witnesses [martyrs] to these things, and so also is the Holy Spirit whom God has given to those who obey Him."* The more you obey His instructions, the more He sees your faithfulness, and He will reward you. How does He reward your faithfulness? He rewards you with more work…because He trusts you.

HOW TO WALK IN MORE ANOINTING

One of the greatest requirements for more of Jesus and His anointing is to hunger and thirst for more of Him, to desire to know Him intimately. In Matthew 5:6, the promise for that desire is, "*…you shall be filled.*" Many years ago, while I was teaching on the subject of the anointing in a church in Asia, a young man attended every class, sitting in the back row, listening with purpose, and taking copious notes. At the end of the teaching, he would come up to me and say, "Sister Flo, I want the same anointing that is on you to come on me for my ministry." The Lord told him through a prophetic word that he would pastor 900 people in his church.

I would tell him, "Brother, keep coming to the class. Keep coming, for the anointing is caught when you are taught." Toward the end of the week, I told the students and the host church that we would have a special service on Friday night for an impartation of the anointing. When Friday came, I locked myself in my room and prayed all day, asking the Lord what I was to speak on for that special service. He told me to speak on the "Tallit of Glory," a teaching about the Jewish mantle or the prayer shawl that fell from Elijah to Elisha. (I have been teaching on the tallit since the early '90s.)

160

While praying for the service, my thoughts went to the young man who was so hungry for the anointing to come upon his ministry. His holy aspirations stirred me to pray more that day. I starting meditating about the tallit of glory or the Jewish prayer shawl, and I saw in my mind's eye that I was going to throw that mantle on that young preacher just like Elijah of old threw it on Elisha (see 1 Kings 19:19). That was what *I* was planning to do, but I was not aware that it was not what the *Lord* was planning to do.

As I continued to pray (with ear phones on, listening to Christian worship), the thought came to me to look up the Scripture where Paul the apostle anointed *"handkerchiefs or aprons;"* when these prayer cloths were laid upon the sick, *"...the diseases left them and the evil spirits went out of them"* (Acts 19:11-12). I had this wild thought that, if the anointing was perceptible by touch in Paul's ministry, the anointing could be tangible in my ministry, so I lifted up the tallit of glory (or the mantle) before the Lord and asked Him to anoint it so that I could throw it over this young pastor. All of a sudden, my hands began to vibrate, and I could literally feel the anointing of God going into that prayer shawl. When I sensed that the transfer of power was over, I threw it over my head, and bam! Down I went. My forehead hit the floor, my elbows touched the floor, and my knees buckled under the weight of glory. I was "stuck" (I could not move) in that position for about 30 minutes as I wept before the Lord.

The cassette music went into auto rewind, and I still could not get up. When I finally could move, it was with great effort that I got dressed for the service. My armor-bearer, or assistant, had to steady me to get me into the car and into the church. She escorted me to the front row; and after worship, the pastor introduced me.

Because I am Native American, he would introduce me as either "Dances with Wolves" or "Pocahontas." I think on that particular night he called me "Dances with Wolves." I went up to the platform and looked out over the audience. The packed-out auditorium had no room left. Hungry saints had taken every space in the church. They were jammed in there like sardines in a can. I thought, *I should not have announced this special service because so many came that did not attend the weekly teaching sessions on the anointing, but I promised to lay hands on everyone.*

Sensing the presence of the Lord and a surge of His joy, I opened in prayer and started into my message. I got to the place in the Word where Elijah, caught up by the whirlwind, dropped his mantle for Elisha to pick up. (The particular Jewish prayer mantle that I used that night was made of 100% wool, so it was heavy.) As I was making the point about the whirlwind (I had no intention of doing this), I spontaneously threw the tallit of glory upward. It shot up 30 feet into the air, and then right in midair, it turned at a 90 degree angle and shot toward the front row right where I had been sitting. To my surprise, that young pastor who had always sat in the back row was now sitting in my chair, and the mantle of glory hit him and landed on his right shoulder! (The Lord threw that mantle at him!) His eyes opened wide, and his mouth flew open, but no sound came out. I stared at him in almost disbelief and said to the audience, "There is no need to continue preaching, the anointing is here *now!* Everyone who wants the anointing, line up." And they did. The ushers had them in formation around the building and then moved the overflow crowd on to the upper three floors! Because under the anointing you always do everything better, I had no problem climbing those stairs to lay hands on the people. I had such energy from the Lord. What a night that was!

A Necktie Holds the Anointing

When I lived in Alaska, Pastor Mike scheduled Mario Murillo to do a citywide crusade in one of our major cities. When I heard about it, I was so disappointed that I would not have the unique opportunity to sit under Mario Murillo's anointing because of a conflict in my schedule. I had previously booked some meetings in another state during the week Evangelist Murillo was to be in our city. About a week before the Mario Murillo Crusade, the committee chairman called me and asked if he could use my white Cadillac to escort Mario to and from the meetings, and of course, I said yes. I told my husband Mike about my car, and he said I could do it on one condition—he wanted one of Mario's neckties. Then Mike smiled and said, "Who knows what might happen!"

Well, just before I left on my ministry trip, I typed a letter to Mario telling him what my husband Mike said and included a $75 check to replace the tie he would give to Mike. I gave the letter with the enclosed check and my car keys to the committee chairman. Two days before I left on my trip, Mike had a dream about Brother Murillo. In the dream, Mike was driving Mario around, and when he went to pick up him up, Mario started to get into the back seat of my car. When Mike saw that, he jumped out of the car, grabbed Mario by the necktie, and started pulling him into the front seat. When Mike told me the dream, I said to him, "You sure must want that necktie."

When I arrived back home from my trip, the first question I asked Mike was about that necktie. He said that the committee chairman had returned my car but that there was no tie. I was ticked off and said, "I am going to write to Mario and ask for my $75 back!"

Mike said in his usual kind manner, "Never mind Flo." A couple days later, I was working in my office when Mike came home from the post office with our mail. I ignored him because I was very preoccupied with what I was typing on my computer. But when I heard him tear open a package, I immediately sensed *something*, so I turned to look at what he was opening. The moment he pulled that necktie out of the package, the power of God hit me, and I was instantly Acts 2 drunk!

When Mike saw how it affected me, he got this glint in his eye, came over to me, and started playfully hitting me with that tie. The more he hit me on the head, the more I slid off my chair! I squealed and said, "Boy, are you going to be fun to travel with!" When I regained my composure, we read the enclosed letter: "Dear Flo, as per your request here is my most anointed tie—be sure to have a catcher nearby when the man puts this on! The meetings in Alaska were marvelous but way too short—I can't wait to return. Love, Mario Murillo." Then Mike took a closer look at the tie and said, "Look at this, he even sent it with his gravy stain on it." Nevertheless, I could tell he was pleased to have that tie.

When Mike went out of town on union business, he said to me, "Don't touch my tie!" While he was gone, I decided to attend a local church where a friend of mine pastored. Even though Mike said not to touch his tie, I could not resist, so I took it out of the drawer and put it on. It is a beautiful, brightly-colored silk tie with tongues of fire on it! As I held it, I could feel the tangible anointing in it. The second I put it around my neck, I was again drunk in the Lord. This is amazing, Lord! I got dressed and went to church. During the service, my pastor-friend asked if anyone had a testimony to share, so I got up and told about the tie. While Pastor Daymond was listening to me, he started laughing; he was almost falling off his chair, he was laughing so hard. The joy then hit the congregation, and we were all happy. It was a joy unspeakable and full of glory!

ENDNOTES

1. *Merriam-Webster's Collegiate Dictionary*, 11th edition, s.v. "Inherent."

2. *Ibid*, s.v. "Manifest."

3. Finis Jennings Dake, *Dake Annotated Reference Bible* (Lawrenceville, GA: Dake Publishing, 1999), commentary notes from John 3:34, p.96.

4. *Merriam-Webster's*, s.v. "Martyr."

5. James Strong, *The New Strong's Expanded Exhaustive Concordance of the Bible* (Nashville, TN: Thomas Nelson, 2001); "Greek Dictionary," *dierchomai*, number 1330.

Chapter 7

SPIRITUAL PERCEPTION

Likewise the Spirit also helps in our weaknesses, for we do not know what we should pray for as we ought, but the Spirit Himself makes intercession for us with groaning which cannot be uttered. Now He who searches the hearts knows what the mind of the Spirit is, because He makes intercession for the saints according to the will of God (Romans 8:26-27).

The Holy Spirit listens to Heaven's dialogue regarding your life and your ministry. He knows what Father has planned for you. As He hears, He begins to reveal God's plan to your heart. As *you* listen to the Holy Spirit, He will begin to unfold a plan about you that will take you beyond what you thought could happen, but you can only discover this plan by revelation as you pray in tongues.

Praying in tongues is the gateway to the supernatural. Jude 1:20 says, *"But you, beloved, building yourselves up on your most holy faith, praying in the Holy Spirit."* As you pray in tongues, you are building yourself up in mountain-moving faith that can overcome any obstacle in life. The Amplified Bible says, in this verse, that you are rising up like an edifice or a magnificent structure, strong and powerful.

As you present your body as a holy living sacrifice, it will be pleasing to God (see Rom. 12:1). In Romans 12:2, we are told to renew our minds to think as God thinks; then we will know the *"…good and acceptable and perfect will of God."*

The Lord does not have three wills for your life. Proverbs 4:18 says, *"The path* [not paths] *of the just is like the shining sun that shines ever brighter unto the perfect day."* There is only one path for the righteous—the way of holiness.

During times of praying in tongues, the revelation of His will comes to our hearts and minds. First Corinthians 14:14 declares, *"For if I pray in a tongue, my spirit prays, but my understanding is unfruitful. What is the conclusion then? I will pray with the spirit, and I will also pray with the understanding."* Something supernatural takes places as you are praying in tongues—your spirit opens up to God's Spirit, and the Lord begins to talk to your spirit: *"He who searches the heart knows what the mind of the Spirit is"* (Rom. 8:27). Something deep is happening. Romans 8:26-27 indicates that as you pray in tongues the Holy Spirit *"makes intercession for the saints* [that includes you!] *according to the will of God."* First

Corinthians 14:2 reveals that *"He who speaks in a tongue does not speak to men but to God, for no one understands him; however, in the spirit he speaks mysteries."* The Holy Spirit will then bring those mysteries that you have been praying before the throne of God and release them back to you through your spiritual perception. If you are one who takes notes, this would be a good time to write down what the Holy Spirit reveals during times of intercession. He not only unveils mysteries so that they are no longer a mystery; He will also reveal Father's plans.

Write these revelations down, and keep a log of the things He says to you.

The Godhead wants to speak to your spirit man. Luke 16:19-31 gives us the narration of the rich man and Lazarus. In the story both of them die. Lazarus goes to a beautiful heavenly place while the rich man goes to a place of torment: *"And being in torments in Hades,* [the rich man] *lifted up his eyes and saw..."* (Luke 16:23). This man's "spirit man" had eyes and intense feelings. *"...he lifted up his eyes and saw...."* Your spirit man has spiritual perception as well. It is to *this* "spirit man" that the Holy Spirit speaks those *mysteries*.

The Holy Spirit can communicate several ways with your spirit:

1. Through the heavens: *"The heavens declare* [or recount] *the glory of God; and the firmament sheweth his handywork"* (KJV). In Matthew 2:7-9, it says that the star led the wise men to where Jesus was.

2. Through an inner witness: First John 2:20 speaks of the "believer's anointing" through which we hear accurately what the Holy Spirit is saying to us. *"But you have an anointing from the Holy One, and you know all things."*

3. Through an audible voice: Many times in the Bible, the audible voice of the Lord was heard by His prophets. For example, in First Samuel 3, the Lord called Samuel in an audible voice three times.

4. Through the Word of God: Hebrews 4:12 says, *"For the word of God is living and powerful, and sharper than any two-edged sword, piercing even to the division of soul and spirit, and of joints and marrow, and is a discerner of the thoughts and intents of the heart."*

5. Through people: In First Corinthians 12-14, we learn about the use of the gifts of the Spirit through the believers.

6. Through current events: If you go back in history, you can trace the dealings of God with the nation of Israel. Time after time, immediately after those events, something major happened in the Body of Christ. Prophets watch current events to hear what the Holy Spirit is saying to His Church. *"He who has an ear, let him hear what the Spirit says to the churches"* (Rev. 2:7).

7. Through revelation or spiritual perception: Many of the prophets of old received revelation this way, *"And the word of the Lord came unto Abram in a vision saying…"* (Gen. 15:1).

8. Through visions: Acts 22:17 says, *"Now it happened, when I returned to Jerusalem and was praying in the temple, that I was in a trance and saw Him saying to me, 'Make haste and get out of Jerusalem quickly; for they will not receive your testimony concerning Me."*

9. Through dreams: Job 33:14-16 says, *"For God may speak in one way, or in another, yet man does not perceive it. In a dream, in a vision of the night, when deep sleep falls*

upon men, while slumbering on their beds, then He opens the ears of men, and seals their instruction."

A Woman Tries to Kill Me

Staying prayed up and living by spiritual perception will save your life. Many years ago, I went to visit some friends in Canada. When I arrived in their home, I sensed something was wrong, and noticed my friend did not look quite right. In the Spirit, I could perceive darkness on her face. I immediately began to talk silently to the Lord about this, and I continued to observe her actions and her countenance all afternoon. I queried her in a subtle way about her recent spiritual activities, and she told me that she was continuing with her deliverance ministry. Over the years, I noticed my friend was preoccupied with dealing with demons and doing deliverance on people, and it troubled me that her ministry seemed unbalanced. Knowing the spirit realm as I do, I was concerned for her welfare.

The next morning, she had to go out, so I went with her, and we had light conversation until we returned to her home. I continued to see that darkness on her, and some of the things that she shared with me left me suspect of her mental health. When we returned home, she made some snacks for an early dinner. After eating, she sat in the far corner of her living room knitting a garment with barely enough light to see what she was doing. She sat in total silence in the dim light with her head down while her husband, a jovial man, talked and laughed with me. I kept my eye on her, but she never looked up. While we were laughing, she interrupted us and said in a low guttural voice, "When you came here, you were depressed and had a spirit of suicide on you, and now that spirit has jumped on me!"

I sat at first stunned by her comment until the Holy Spirit said to me in a firm voice, "She is planning on killing you tonight! Engage in a conversation with her, and act as if you do not see that demon on her. After 15 minutes, excuse yourself; tell them you are tired and are going to bed." I tried not to swallow big or open my eyes in shock for fear that demon would know I had perceived his presence. I sat there calm on the outside but trembling on the inside. I said to her that I did not have a spirit of suicide on me when I came, but she was convinced in her mind there was. Those 15 minutes seemed more like an hour and 15 minutes, but when 15 minutes had passed, I excused myself as instructed and went to my room.

I did not get undressed but lay still on my bed staring at the ceiling for several hours. There was no chance that I was going to go to sleep now. The hours ticked by slowly as I lay wide-awake, waiting for my next instruction. Finally, at 2 A.M., the Holy Spirit spoke and told me to pack my personal belongings and write her a "Thank you" note for her "hospitality." After thanking her for letting me stay in her home, I put it in the envelope and laid it on the bed.

I grabbed my bag and then had a frightening thought. On the long drive to her home, I had encountered engine trouble and had to stop at a garage to get it fixed. The garage attendant told me that I needed to get my engine serviced as soon as I got home. I said to the Lord, "What if my engine stalls when I try to back out of her driveway?" There was no answer, so I quietly tiptoed through the living room and put my hand on the locked door. My stomach became tight, and my heart started to pound as I unlocked the door. Instinctively, I knew in my spirit that the demon was about to wake her up, so I quickened my steps to my car. *O good, it is not frozen.* I got into the car and put the key in the ignition; with a prayer, I turned the key, and to my relief, it started.

I backed the car out of the carport, put it in drive, and hit the gas pedal. My hands were shaking, and my palms were wet with sweat. It was still dark, but thank God, I was on my way. Then I saw a sign in the distance, and as I approached, I saw that it read, "Dead End." "Dead End! O Jesus!" I cried out, "I went in the wrong direction!" I quickly found a place to turn around and hit the gas pedal again. I drove for quite a distance, and then I finally noticed that I was nearing the border. *Wonderful!* However, I continued to sense some demonic force following me. My mind left that thought when I spotted a small grocery store and remembered how much my husband loves Canadian butter, so I stopped my car to purchase a couple of pounds.

Here my friend was planning to kill me, a demon was following me, and I stopped for two pounds of butter for my husband! Visibly shaken, I walked into the store. The cashier looked at me with a curious look when I said in a loud voice, "Where is the butter?" I can just imagine what I looked like to this poor man. I am sure I frightened him. I bought two pounds and hurried out the door. I felt like running in my spirit because I could not get away from this "thing" that was following me. I passed the security guard, and he waved me toward the border. Just as I was driving over the border into the United States, the demonic force suddenly left my car, as if it did not want to cross over the line.

I pondered this for a few moments, and then I remembered the story in the Bible when Jesus cast "legion" out of the demon-possessed man of the country of the Gadarenes. That demon begged Jesus *"…he besought Him much that he would not send them away out of the country"* (Mark 5:10). Some demons are territorial and like certain areas more than others. I believe that is why we have gang wars. The stronger demons guard "their" areas. I can only assume, based on this portion of Scripture, that when I crossed over into the U.S., the demon that was following me had no right to be in our territory. After many hours of driving, I finally arrived home a little tired but so glad to be safe. Mike greeted me at the door with a very troubled look on his face. He asked me why my friend was so upset. He said he had called that morning, and she told Mike that I had left in the middle of the night; he could tell she was very angry with me. He cut the conversation short and waited for me to arrive home. Later that day, I received a call from my intercessor Mary from Alaska, and she was so excited I could barely understand her. She repeated herself and told me that the Lord had awakened her to pray for me because someone was going to try to kill me! *"Two will put 10,000 to flight..."* (see Deuteronomy 32:30).

It pays to stay prayed up and in tune with the Holy Spirit so you can discern in your spirit all the spiritual forces around you. The spiritual world is just as real as our world. You cannot see those spirits unless the Lord opens your spirit eyes to them. On a clear night, you can see with your natural eyes all the thousands of stars in the sky. When the morning rays of the sun come over the horizon, you can no longer see those stars, but you know they are there. As you continue to listen to the Holy Spirit, He will lead you to safety because He sees everything and knows everything.

PROPHETIC WORD FOR SCOTLAND

In preparation for my trip to the United Kingdom, I spent quality time praying in the spirit, interceding in tongues for the meetings. At 8:10 A.M., May 21, 1993, the Lord spoke to my inner woman and gave me a prophetic word for the nation of Scotland. What I heard in my heart came from my spirit, and it was the desire of the Father for that country. He then told me not to release the prophecy until He instructed me. When my traveling companion and I arrived in Scotland in July, our host pastor took us to a large Charismatic church and introduced us.

> While I was greeting the people, I silently asked the Lord if this was the time, and He said clearly, "No," so I kept the written word in my pocket.

The next morning our hosts escorted us to a church housed in a castle where several local leaders had gathered for prayer. As the meeting progressed, the brothers began to go from pastor to pastor, expressing their strong desire for revival. When the meeting concluded, one of the pastors asked if we had anything to share. I looked at Sheila, and she indicated that she did not have anything at that time, so I asked the Lord, "Is this the time?" He said "Yes." I gave the pastors the background of the prophetic word and began to read it.

The following is the word: "There is a radical reformation coming to this nation. Everything shall be changed. Every life shall be touched, for My glory is about to descend, and My river is about to rush forth. Many will cry out flood warnings…for it is coming…and it is about to wash the land of years of filth. Then a new move shall begin. For I AM that I AM, and there is no other. I speak no careless word. That which I have promised shall happen. Scotland shall stand and see My glory and My power. I shall flood this nation with miracles, and My servants shall do many signs and many wonders. Those who have stood all these years are about to see the reward of the wicked, but also the reward of the righteous, for I shall reward the work of their hands."

The Lord went on to say, "Tell them to get ready…for the flood shall come in the first stage in the year of our Lord—1993—first in July, then October, then November. By 1994, they shall be in flood stage. A river too deep to cross over, and wherever the river flows many shall be healed, and everything shall live, saith the Lord of Hosts."

The pastors sat in complete silence for a long minute—some just staring at me while others had their eyes closed in quiet contemplation. Then a young minister named Pastor Martin said to me, "Reread the first line again." Before I began, he told us about a reoccurring vision he has had of the coming revival to Scotland and a magazine entitled *A New Reformation* declaring the mighty works of God. When he finished speaking, I reread the first line, "There is a radical reformation coming to this nation…" When I said that, the power of God hit Pastor Martin and his friend Pastor David, and they fell to the floor, rolled up in a fetal position, and began to laugh uncontrollably in holy laughter. We all sat there just staring at them in shock. I had been in some of the "holy laughter" meetings in the U.S. prior to coming to the UK, but I never once mentioned to these pastors this move of God. Later, I found out they had never heard of Rodney Howard-Browne or his "laughter" meetings (which was not a laughter revival but a holy revival), so what we witnessed there in that castle had nothing to do with Rodney; it was a holy moment of the Lord Jesus. He just loves to touch His people!

The following night, expectations were high. For the next five nights, the Glory Cloud rolled in, and people were caught up in trances, or fell on the floor laughing; the building shook by the power of God, and some could not speak in English for hours. All this happened because of a prophetic word received through revelation or spiritual perception and released in God's perfect timing!

During one of the nights that I ministered, I felt the weight of glory so heavy; I was moving in slow motion, and my speech was slurred. My whole body was enveloped in Him; I felt like I was going to step into another realm of glory—something heavenly and very, very holy. I believe there are realms of glory yet unknown to the casual believer, but as the Church presses into a greater intimacy with Jesus, His presence will come in wave after wave of glory and power to set the captives free.

The next night, my friend Reverend Sheila ministered the Word. When she was finished preaching, I heard Pastor Martin yell out, "Sister Sheila, stand up and receive the word of the Lord." I was standing in the back of the building watching her when that prophetic word hit her. She bolted upwards at least a foot and fell on her back! I thought, *Now that is a true prophetic word from God. It has power! Not, "O I love you my children" and "I long for you" or some generic word.* As I continued standing awestruck, I saw the anointing come down on those big Scottish men, and they began flipping over their chairs onto the floor with no catchers. The move of God went on for days, and the building was packed out. One night, the small room was so packed that we had to have the people stand, and Pastor Martin and I stepped on to the chairs going up and down the aisles behind the people laying hands on their heads.

Later that year, in November 1994, I took another team back to the UK, and we saw the next wave of revival in signs, wonders, and miracles. One night, two pastors got so drunk on the new wine (Acts 2 *"these are not drunken as you suppose..."*) that they were beside themselves in outrageous joy, unable to speak in English; others had to be carried home; and the holy rollers were back. Revival had come to Scotland.

KNOWING YOUR CALLING

The more you yield to Jesus, the more you are filled with His Presence, the more He will use you. I like what a minister friend always said, "Whatever He can get in you will flow through you." To flow fully in the anointing, you must know where He has placed you; that is, your position in the Body of Christ. As you learn what He has called *you* to do, you will walk in a greater authority to get the job done. If He has called you into full-time ministry and you are the janitor in the church, you will always feel disharmonious and out-of-joint and rob the Body of Christ of that anointing. To know your calling, you must spend time with Jesus in His Word, adoring Him and praying in tongues. Romans 12:4 says, *"For as we have many members in one body, but all the members do not have the same function...."*

I knew of a powerful and effective intercessor that could shake Heaven when she prayed. She would go from house to house, praying for people, and the Lord flowed through her in miracle-working power. One day, *she* decided to go outside the border of her calling and anointing, and she entered into an area that she was not called to. Because she used to intercede for a prophetic minister who had an Ephesians 4:11 pulpit calling, she desired to have that same pulpit calling as well. She quit praying for the one the Lord had called her to intercede for and entered into "her" missionary ministry. From the day she stood in the pulpit *outside of her calling and anointing,* she began to die physically and eventually passed from this earth. When the books of Heaven are opened, she will weep because she did not fulfill *her* ministry.

The Ministry Gifts

First Corinthians 12:27-28 lists the different ministry gifts in a divine order: *"Now you are the body of Christ, and members individually. And God has appointed these in the church: first apostles, second prophets, third teachers, after that miracles, then gifts of healings, helps, administrations, varieties of tongues."* You will find your ministry somewhere in that roster. Regardless of where you are on that list, all members of the Body should flow in the anointing of God with the gifts listed in First Corinthians 12. Verse 7 tells us succinctly, *"the manifestation of the Spirit is given to each one...."* In other words, if called as a prophet, you should flow in the gifts of that office; if called as the janitor in the church, you should flow in the gifts as well—for the manifestation is given to all, even to 10-year-old children and 90-year-old grandmothers.

Ephesians 4:11-12 lists the five-fold ministers. *"And He Himself gave some to be apostles, some prophets, some evangelists, and some pastors and teachers, for the equipping of the saints for the work of ministry...."* The word *some* is the Greek word *ho*, which includes the feminine.[1]

Great Revelation Coming to Five-Fold Ministers

There is coming great revelation of the glory of the Son of God to the "shepherds" or the five-fold ministers who have been *faithfully* tending the flock of God—in the good times and the bad times. In Luke 2:8-20, it says that there were *"shepherds living out in the fields, keeping watch over their flock by night...."* Let's look at the possible symbolism of this passage. The word *night* is the midnight hour, which is symbolic of the end of the age, a change in time, and a time of new beginning. We are in that season now. The shepherds (or pastors or leaders) in the field saw the fullness of God's glory as it *"shone around them."* That glory was the seven Spirits of God mentioned in Revelation 3:1. In the last days, the Bible says this glory covers the earth, but it is the *"knowledge of the glory"* (Hab. 2:14) that is unknown to humanity. This knowledge will come through the character and the actions of the sons of God. As the fivefold ministers of God receive the fullness of the Glory revelation and teach it to the Body of Christ, the sons and daughters of the Lord will in turn release the knowledge of the Glory to the world in signs, wonders, and miracles. Then *"...the earth will be filled with the knowledge of the Glory of the Lord, as the waters cover the sea"* (Hab. 2:14).

DESCRIPTION OF FIVEFOLD MINISTERS

At the risk of oversimplifying, the apostle is one sent by God; the prophet is one who speaks for God; the evangelist is a bearer of the Good News; the shepherd is our brother's keeper; and the teacher is the one who is able to instruct in the ways of God. The primary work of each of these ministry gifts is to train and equip the saints to do the work of *their* ministry. The apostle is to govern; the prophet is to guide; the evangelist is to go; the pastor is to guard; and the teacher is to ground (in the Word).

First Corinthians 12 teaches us about the diversity in the Body of Christ. Verses 15-18 give us a description of the fivefold ministry gifts:

> *If the foot should say, "Because I am not a hand, I am not of the body," is it therefore not of the body? And if the ear should say, "Because I am not an eye, I am not of the body," is it therefore not of the body? If the whole body were an eye, where would be the hearing? If the whole were hearing,*

where would be the smelling? But now God has set the members, each one of them, in the body just as He pleased.

The *foot* is the evangelist. He is the one who goes out the farthest. He takes the Good News to the world and to the church. The *hand* is the pastor-shepherd who lovingly helps and assists believers with their ministry. He shares with the sheep what God is saying on a daily basis. The *foot* and the *hand* sometimes are suspicious of one another, but these two ministry gifts need each other to build the Kingdom of God in the local church. The *ear* is the prophet who hears what God is saying and speaks it forth, usually with great passion. The eye is the apostle who sees the whole picture. The apostles are sent out on specific missions releasing authority or credentials to build the Church.

Just as the church began with apostolic authority, so it shall be in the last day. The *nose* is the teacher who sniffs out or discerns what is wrong and what is needed to bring the Body back into balance. These fivefold ministry gifts are likened to the five ingredients of the anointing oil. When operating under *that* fullness, every enslaving yoke breaks off the believers so they can go out doing the works of Christ and evangelizing the world.

First Corinthians 12:27-28 goes on to list the ministry of *helps,* which is the gifting to invest in the life of the church in any area where help is needed. The ministry of *administrations* describes the organizational skills needed in the government of the local church. The *varieties of tongues,* along with the other seven functions listed in this passage are the foundation for the operation of the church.

The "Untouchables" Become Evangelists

Each gift, chosen, called, and equipped by Christ Himself, is for the edification of the Body of Jesus. We sometimes do not like the person that God has chosen for a certain gifting because of ethnicity or gender or background, but our opinion matters little. If God chooses them and there is an anointing upon their life and ministry, then God has approved them. Do you recall the demon-possessed man out of whom Jesus cast a legion of demons? Luke 8:38-39 says, *"Now the man from whom the demons had departed begged Him that he might be with Him. But Jesus sent him away, saying 'Return to your own house, and tell what great things God has done for you.'"* After Jesus cast the demons out of this man, the Bible says that he was in his right mind, clothed, and sitting at Jesus' feet. After this man was set free, he wanted to travel with Jesus, but Jesus did not permit him. Just because you have been set free and filled with an anointing does not mean you should go behind a pulpit and start preaching. There is a place for everyone who is anointed. Jesus told him to go and be an evangelist right where he lived. Mark 5:20 says of this man (who most people would neither want in their church nor ordain in their organization), *"he departed and began to publish in Decapolis how great things Jesus had done for him: and all men did marvel."*

Women Leaders

The Lord elaborated a well-known portion of Scripture to me in a prophetic light. It was the story of the woman, in Matthew 26:6-13, who broke the alabaster flask of very costly oil; the Bible says she *"poured it on His head...."* When the disciples saw this extravagance poured out on Jesus, they were indignant at what they considered a waste, but Jesus rebuked them and told them to leave her alone. He said, *"For in pouring this fragrant oil on My body, she did it for My burial."* She knew He would rise again, so she poured the oil on Him before He lay in the tomb. The Bible clearly tells us she poured it on His head, but Jesus said she poured it on His *body*, and then He finishes by telling the brothers, *"She has done a good work for Me."* The Lord showed me that the Body of Christ would not operate in the fullness of power until the women are allowed to pour out the oil (which is the anointing) on His Body, and when they do, it will be, as He said, *"a good work."*

BODY MINISTRY

In His explanation of the parable of the tares, Jesus told His disciples that the harvest (of souls) is the end of the age (see Matt. 13:36-43). As the anointing increases to bring in the lost, it will take the cooperation of all believers, regardless of denomination, gender, ethnicity, or title. The Holy Spirit gives us a profound picture of the last day's revival in Luke 5:1-11: *"...the multitude pressed about Him* [Jesus] *to hear the Word of God...."* That is a sign of a true revival—when the masses want to hear the Word. Before Jesus preached, he saw two boats, *"and He got into one of the boats..."* (Luke 5:3). Jesus is about to chose His new leaders for the 21st century. Maybe He is about to step into your boat!

After He preached, He told Peter (whose boat Jesus was preaching from) to *"launch out into the deep and let down your nets for a catch"* (Luke 5:4). Peter protested, telling Jesus he had been toiling all night long and had caught nothing. Do you sometimes feel that way? You have done everything you know to do, and yet you have nothing to show for your efforts. Peter may have thought, *You are the carpenter, and I am the fisherman, and **You** are telling me how to fish!* Nevertheless, Peter did not say what he was thinking. He told Jesus, *"We have toiled all* *night and caught nothing; nevertheless at Your word I will let down the net"* (Luke 5:5). When Peter obeyed, he caught so many fish that the net was breaking, so he signaled to his brothers and partners (or other ministers or ministries) in the other boat to come and help him. When they came to his rescue, they *"filled both boats and began to sink"* (Luke 5:7).

When Peter saw that, he fell down before Jesus and said, "Depart from me, for I am a sinful man, O Lord" (Luke 5:8). What was Peter's sin? He disobeyed the Lord's instructions. Jesus told him to "let down your nets…" (plural), but Peter only let down one net, and the sad fact is that they lost some of the catch!

> Peter's sin was disobedience, for *partial obedience is disobedience*. Even after the other boat came, it was not enough, for both boats began to sink. It will take all of us to bring in the big catch. After this lesson, the goodness of Jesus was expressed to Peter when He told him, *"Do not be afraid. From now on you will catch men"* (Luke 5:10).

SEEING AS GOD SEES

Mark 8:22-25 tells the story of a blind man healed by Jesus. I realize this account is about physical healing, but I see it with prophetic eyes. The story begins when a blind man brought to Jesus in the city of Bethsaida begs Him to touch him. Jesus takes the blind man by the hand and leads him out of the city. He applies spit on his eyes, puts His hands on him, and asks if he sees anything. He looks up and says, *"I see men like trees walking"*(Mark 8:24). His spiritual perception is off, so Jesus touches his eyes again, *"…and made him look up…"* (Mark 8:25).

The only way you will see men as God sees them is to look up into the face of Jesus; otherwise, you will see with religious eyes. After Jesus put His hand on him a second time, *"he was restored and saw everyone clearly"* (Mark 8:25). We, like this blind man, are a work in progress. We have to look with God's eyes of love to have the right spiritual perception of those around us, especially those who are not like us.

Even after this teaching, the resurrected Christ had to come to the disciples again to help them understand how much He loves *all* humanity. In Acts 10:9-48, Jesus speaks to Peter while he is in a trance on the rooftop waiting for his host to prepare a noonday meal. In this vision, Peter sees all kinds of animals, birds, and reptiles—some clean, some unclean. Jesus says to Peter, *"Rise, Peter; kill and eat"* (Acts 10:13). Peter, being a good Jew, was taught not to eat anything unclean, but Jesus is commanding him to eat. He tells him three times, and three times Peter resists the Lord's commands. While Peter is contemplating the vision, three Gentile men from Cornelius' house (a Roman) sent for Peter.

At the Lord's instruction, Peter went with them. If the Lord had not prepared him, through the vision, to go the house of a Gentile, he never would have gone. When Peter arrives at Cornelius' home, he tells him, *"You know how unlawful it is for a Jewish man to keep company with or go to one of another nation. But God has shown me that I should not call any man common or unclean"* (Acts 10:28). After the Lord broke down Peter's prejudice and pride, he learned from God's perspective that all men are created in God's likeness and are equally loved by Him.

Sometimes we are not fully aware of our prejudices or anything that is dark in us until the light of the Gospel shines upon it.

Proverbs 20:27 tells us, *"The spirit of man is the candle of the Lord, searching all the inward parts of the belly."* The Holy Spirit searches all the dark parts in our hearts that need the truth. The "candle" of your spirit was lit when you were born again; moreover, when you read the Word of God and pray in tongues, that candle grows brighter.

In Second Corinthians 10:4-6, Paul writes, *"For the weapons of our warfare are not carnal but mighty in God for pulling down strongholds, casting down arguments and every high thing that exalts itself against the knowledge of God, bringing every thought into captivity to the obedience of Christ…."* When we were born again, our spirits came alive, but our minds, our thought patterns, our arguments, and our theories came into conflict with anything that was of God. The Holy Spirit wants to end every thought pattern that has caused us hurt or pain and failure. Romans 8:12-13 tells us how to end this cycle of defeat in our minds: *"Therefore, brethren, we are debtors—not to the flesh, to live according to the flesh. For if you live according to the flesh you will die; but if **by the Spirit** you put to death the deeds of the body, you will live."* Some things are too strong for us to handle on our own.

If you listen to the reasoning of your soul, it will sabotage you. Your soul is your mind, will, and emotions. Once you start that destructive behavior, you will begin a cycle of defeat. Your negative thought life runs on a train track. If you step on the track with a negative thought and do not put a stop to that kind of thinking quickly, you will go around and around; soon you will be unable to get off. When that happens, a stronghold has taken root, and it is not easily uprooted. Verse 27 of that same chapter says, "*Now He who searches the hearts knows what the mind of the Spirit is, because He makes intercession for the saints according to the will of God.*" To counteract an internal war, you need to fight in the spirit. That is why it is so important to pray in tongues, because the Holy Spirit goes for the root, not the bad fruit. Then "*...all things work together for good...*" in your life (Rom. 8:28).

When I was first born-again in the early '70s, I use to be shy and very withdrawn. I saw myself as a victim of society, discarded, unwanted, unaccepted, and unloved, until one day the Holy Spirit spoke to me about Jesus' deep, abiding love for me. When I heard those words of love, I could hardly believe that Jesus loved me that much. I asked Him, "You mean You love *me* as much as you love Billy Graham?" His affirmations that afternoon set me on a new course of healing, bringing me to the place where I knew I was loved, wanted, and accepted in the beloved. However, it took years to undo the damage done to my psyche. It took years to bring a total healing to my mind, but when I came out on the other side, I no longer felt like a victim but a victor.

In the process of ending destructive habits through the power of the Holy Spirit, you must first be truthful.

No light can come into the dark areas of your soul until you are first truthful with yourself and with the Lord. I have found that, when I allow the Lord to deal with me in the depth of my soul, He is always kind and gentle yet profoundly penetrating. His purpose is always to bring me to wholeness.

In Ephesians 6:11-14, Paul begins to describe the spiritual war at hand and our need for the *"whole armor of God."* The first piece of armor in Paul's list is the truth that girds the waist. *Truth* in verse 14 means "to be true (in doctrine and profession), to speak (tell) the truth."[1] Only as we are truthful or honest Christians, with integrity, can we defeat the father of lies.

> *Finally, my brethren, be strong in the Lord and in the power of His might. Put on the whole armor of God, that you may be able to stand against the wiles of the devil. For we do not wrestle against flesh and blood, but against principalities, against powers, against the rulers of the darkness of this age, against spiritual hosts of wickedness in the heavenly places. Therefore, take up the whole armor of God, that you may be able to withstand in the evil day, and having done all, to stand. Stand therefore, having girded your waist with truth...*

Alexander Solzhenitsyn, the Russian philosopher, said, "Truth at its first appearing is always negative." That is true.

Our carnal, fleshly mind will always fight against the Word, but if we will embrace the Word, obey the Word, apply the Word to our lives, no matter how painful, we will walk in the *"abundant life"* Jesus promised us.

ENDNOTES

1. James Strong, *The New Strong's Expanded Exhaustive Concordance of the Bible* (Nashville, TN: Thomas Nelson, 2001); "Greek Dictionary," *ho*, number 3588.

2. Strong, "Greek Dictionary," *aletheuo*, number 226.

Chapter 8

ANGELS IN THE LAST DAYS

The Bible recounts several instances in the Old Testament when angels interacted with God's people. In Genesis 18:1-16, angels talked to and had dinner with Abraham. They announced key events (see Gen. 19), they protected the camp of Israel from an invading army (see Exod. 14:19-20), and they cooked two meals for the prophet Elijah (see 1 Kings 19:5-8). In Judges 13, the angel of the Lord prophesied Samson's birth. These are just a few places where we see angels mentioned in the Old Testament.

Likewise, in the New Testament, we see angels assisting the disciples and making proclamations of historic events. The angel Gabriel was sent from the Lord to Zacharias while he was in the temple to announce the birth of his son John (see Luke 1:13-20). In Acts 5:18-20, the angel of the Lord opened the prison doors for some of the apostles, rescuing them from sure death. In Acts

10:1-7, an angel instructed Cornelius to send for Peter. In Acts 12:7, an angel woke Peter by shaking him. And in Matthew 18:10, the Word tells us that we have guardian angels to watch over us: *"Take heed that you do not despise one of these little ones; for I say to you that in heaven their angels [plural] always see the face of My Father who is in heaven."*

According to this Scripture, we have at least two angels who take care of us, and if we are in full time ministry, we have specific angels to assist us with our work. Some ministers have angels who come with miraculous power, some with great glory, and others who help them flow in the gifts. A prophetic brother and friend told me of an angel assigned to him many years ago; at times, he would show up in meetings, giving this brother information concerning the meeting or those to whom he was about to minister. On the subject of angels, some ministers become fearful or skeptical and avoid the subject altogether. But since they are mentioned *hundreds* of times in the Bible, you are on safe biblical ground not only to study them but also to work with them.

RESCUED BY AN ANGEL

Several years ago, I took a team to another nation on a missionary trip. While we were in that country, some thieves and murderers broke into our compound, ransacked our belongings, raped one of our team members, beat our driver, and put one of the women in the trunk of the car. I was the only one untouched.

Before we went on this trip, some intercessors gave a verbal warning and a prophetic dream to our team that this trip would involve much danger. Despite the warnings, we sensed the Lord was leading us to leave as scheduled. We arrived in that nation without any mishap, but I had a sense of foreboding from the moment we arrived. The morning of the attack, I had a warning dream, and I shared it with my brothers and sisters at the breakfast table and admonished them to be on high alert that day. After breakfast, I had a strong impression that I was to go to my bedroom to pray, and the moment I got on my knees, a spirit of intercession came upon me that broke into spiritual warfare. I prayed for a couple of hours. When the burden of prayer lifted, I had a sense of victory achieved.

From 4 P.M. until late evening, the power kept going out, leaving us without electricity. Our rooms became stifling, so we went out and sit under a tree in the yard to cool off. That night, I asked one of the team to do the Bible study, and when she began, she felt impressed to go around the circle to find out why we had come to this country. Each member told how the Lord had moved circumstances in their ministry for them to come. When it came to my turn, I told them that I did not want to come on this trip but that the Holy Spirit had made it clear to me that I was to go. After our time of prayer, the group started to chit chat, so I excused myself, went to my room, and put on a Christian tape to listen to music and read the Word. At last, our lights had been restored, and my room was starting to cool off.

As I was lying on my stomach on my bed reading the Word, I realized there was a pattern to what the Spirit was saying to me, so I continued to search and ask the Lord questions. Then I read a portion of Scripture, along with my scribbled note in the margin, that said, "No deliverance promised." I asked, "What are you saying to me Lord?" I turned to my Bible again, and He led me to Luke 1:34-35, *"Then Mary said to the angel, 'How can this be, since I do not know a man?' And the angel answered and said to her, 'The Holy Spirit will come upon you, and the power of the Highest will overshadow you...."* That is as far as I got; I was suddenly slain in the spirit—on my bed! I do not know how long I had lain there when I started to hear strong male voices that sounded as if they were coming from 100 miles away. As the sounds got closer, I thought they must have been praying, so I tried to shake myself out of this "spiritual stupor," but I could not do it. Then the voices slowly faded away. Then they came again; this time, they sounded angry, very angry, but again, I could not come out from under this glory. I continued to lay there feeling helpless.

Suddenly, I felt a strong hand shaking me, and someone saying, "Flo, wake up, so-and-so has been raped, they have machine guns, we have been robbed, and they are coming in here next." I tried to tell her that I was not asleep, but under the glory I could not speak. She continued to shake me until she roused me. Jumping off the bed, I instructed her to come with me. I took her to the huge closet, pushed the clothes in front of us, and said, "Pray!" We started to pray in tongues when I heard someone else in trouble. I cried out to the Lord, "O God, what do I do? Should I go out there and help?" He did not answer me.

 When you are in this kind of a crisis, you go by what your inner self tells you. Listen to whatever the Holy Spirit instructs, and follow Him implicitly.

Since He did not give a second command, we stayed in the closet praying in the spirit. About 30 minutes later, I heard the door creaking open, "O God, here they come for us." Before fear could take hold, I heard a whisper, "Flo, come out. It is over now." I opened the door and saw my bold and fearless friend Brenda. We followed her into the living room area where our team had gathered, and we discussed our situation, which was like a terrible nightmare. We prayed, and the Lord comforted us. We consoled and prayed over the woman who had been abused, and the Lord ministered to her in a most wonderful way. After further discussion with the team, we decided to stay for the entire three weeks, knowing we were in the perfect will of the Lord. If we had not had that time of reflection during our Bible study, I think we would have been convinced to leave. During the concluding three weeks, I was almost killed several more times, and in all my years of travel, it was probably the most trying, most horrifying trip of my ministry career.

When I returned home, I called my spiritual mother, Mother Jenkins, and she told me that the night we were attacked, the Lord woke her up and said in a firm voice, "*Get up*, Mary, and pray. Flo is in trouble!" When she got down on her knees, she said to the Lord, "You know that angel with the drawn sword in the Old Testament, well Lord, send that angel and post him as guard in front of Flo's bedroom door." That is exactly what the Lord did, because there was at least an inch and a half gap on the bottom of my door. My room was at the end of a long hallway, so there is no way possible that the robbers and murderers could have not seen the light shining under the threshold of my door unless that angel had blinded them to that light!

My Ministry Angel

In my own ministry, a ministry angel named "Shekinah" has come to my assistance (in a few of my meetings), and when he shows up, the atmosphere and my countenance change dramatically. As I lay hands on people, there is a greater degree of glory and a greater degree of anointing released.

I referred to my ministry angel in the masculine because, in my study on angels in the Bible, they are always masculine in nature, with one exception found in Zechariah 5:9. The angels that guard us must be strong enough to wrestle against the principalities, rulers of darkness, and the spiritual forces in heavenly places. It has been conspicuous to me that the new age stores display their angels as effeminate, as lacking strength or authority. The angels that serve the saints are powerful and not to be taken lightly.

Certainly, in Daniel's experience, the presence of Gabriel produced fear and trembling, *"Suddenly a hand touched me which made me tremble on my knees..."* (Dan. 10:10-12). Then in Acts 27:23-24, an angel appeared before Paul, bringing deliverance to him when he was on a ship caught in a tempest. *"Do not be afraid Paul,"* the angel told him. In most biblical accounts of the appearance of angelic beings, the angels had to tell people not to fear. If they appear in human form, as described in Hebrews 13:2 (*"Do not forget to entertain strangers, for by so doing some have unwittingly entertained angels"*), then of course, there is no reason to fear. If you testified in church, however, that an angel talked to *you*, giving you instructions, most would think you went off the deep end. Whether we believe in them or not, they are real, and they are here to assist us in our lives and ministries.

The assignment of Michael, the archangel, is to the nation of Israel. Gabriel is another archangel sent from the presence of God to certain individuals. These two angels have specific assignments from God, but the angels that you and I might receive a visitation from would probably be angels other than Michael or Gabriel.

Do you realize there was much angelic activity during the first coming of Jesus? God sent the angel Gabriel to Nazareth, to a virgin named Mary, and he told her that she would bear the very Son of God. After Jesus was born, the angels appeared to the shepherds living out in the fields of Israel and proclaimed our Lord's birth. After they made the announcement, they were joined by a multitude of the heavenly host praising God and saying, "*Glory to God in the highest, and on earth peace, goodwill toward men!*" Then they left and returned to Heaven. (See Luke 2:8-15.) It has been noted that when an angel sent by God finishes his mission, he always leaves. I would be suspect if an angel hung around with no purpose but to carry on small talk with me. I have observed in Scripture that, when the ministry angel finishes his assignment, he returns to Heaven, but our guardian angels are with us at all times. On the same note, our guardian angels are there to guard and protect—not to have a conversation with us unless directed by God to do so.

When Jesus was raised back to life after his crucifixion, the angel descended from Heaven and rolled away the stone from the tomb where His body lay. The Bible says that angel's "*countenance was like lightning, and his clothing as white as snow.*" So awesome was his appearance, the guards who were guarding Jesus' tomb shook with fear, and they "*...became like dead men*" (Matt. 28:1-7).

In these last days, there will be as much or more angelic activity for Jesus' second coming as there was during His first coming to earth.

The term *angel* comes from the Greek word *angelos*, which means "messenger." Hebrews 1:13-14 says of the angels: "*But to which of the angels has He ever said, 'Sit at My right hand, till I make Your enemies Your footstool?' Are they* [angels] *not all ministering spirits sent forth to minister for those who will inherit salvation?*" The Bible describes these angels as "*mighty*" (2 Thess. 1:7) and says that they are here to minister to us and for us.

According to the Bible, angels can appear as a light or in human form. Many years ago, the Lord sent an angel from Heaven to assist me, and he appeared to me in human form. It was the late '80s, and I was living in Everett, Washington, with my husband Mike. While living there, an old friend sent an invitation to minister in a church in Grand Forks, British Columbia, Canada, for a week of revival meetings. I was enthusiastic to go and preach the Word—and just as excited to see old friends again. I packed my three red suitcases—one large hard-sided case, one medium-sized case, and a small carry-on—with all I would need for the week, as well as some beautiful gold nugget jewelry that my precious husband Mike had bought for me as a birthday and anniversary gift. I tucked the black velvet case with the gold jewelry in the outside pocket of the carry-on and went to the Seattle airport.

I had made hotel reservations in Vancouver, British Columbia, for a one-night stay and had plans to continue on to Grand Forks, B.C., the next morning. When I arrived at the Vancouver airport that particular evening, the sky was very dark with ominous clouds and pouring down sheets of rain. Because of the lateness of the evening, the airport was almost empty. I stood by the baggage claim carousel waiting for my bags to come down the conveyer belt. There they were, the only three red suitcases and very easy to spot. I picked them up, put them on a cart, and wheeled them out to the cabs waiting outside the terminal. I stopped at the first cab; the driver jumped out, opened up the trunk, and put the two larger suitcases in. He was reaching for my carry-on when I thought to myself, "What am I doing standing out in this rain?" So I immediately opened the back car door and sat down inside. I told him, "Please take me to the Blue Bell Hotel."

When we arrived at the front door of the hotel, he again jumped out, opened my car door, and then went around back to open the trunk. He put my suitcases on a cart and wheeled them into the hotel. I walked up to the front desk and told the desk manager my name, and as he gave me a card to fill out, he asked me if I needed assistance with my suitcases; I told him yes. After I registered, I looked down at my suitcases and noticed that my red carry-on was missing. Just then, I looked up and saw the cab driver going out the front door. I yelled out, "Wait!" but he kept going. I told the hotel agent that he had forgotten to bring in my small carry-on. I asked him to call the cab driver back, so he immediately got on the phone and called the cab company. He said the dispatcher told him that he would contact the cab driver and have him return to the hotel with my carry-on. Several minutes later, the dispatcher called back and told the hotel agent that the cab driver had pulled off the road as soon as he received the call and checked in the trunk of his cab, but the carry-on was not there. I said firmly, "Please call the dispatcher back and tell him I want the cab driver to come to the hotel so I can question him." Again I had to wait several more minutes. The dispatcher called again and reported that the cab driver would not come back to the hotel because he had given me the two suitcases that he had placed in his trunk.

By then, it was getting late, and I had to get to bed to get a good night's rest for the next day's journey, so I said to the hotel agent with a note of agitation in my voice, "Please call the police and tell them what happened." He reluctantly called the police department, and I was instructed to wait in the lobby for an officer to arrive. By the time the officer arrived, it was about 10:30 P.M. When the large-framed officer approached me, he asked the hotel agent for a private room to interview me, and he escorted me to the back office. He asked me to tell my story, and I gave him every detail and then added, "I have thousands of dollars worth of jewelry that my husband has given to me as gifts in a black velvet box tucked in the outside pocket of that red carry-on, and I have to get it back!"

He looked sympathetically at me and said, "I have interviewed the cab driver, and now I have interviewed you—and between you and me, Mrs. Ellers, I believe you. However, you will never be able to convince a judge in a court of law, for it will be your word against his. I am sorry, but I'm afraid your jewelry is lost." I thanked him and thought, *No way! We will see about this.* I went to my room, got on my knees, and prayed, saying to the Lord in closing (which was just a passing thought), ...*and, oh Lord, You know where my bag is, and so I ask you to send an angel to bring it back to me, in Jesus' name, Amen!* With that, I went to bed, and the next morning I went back to the airport and caught my flight to Grand Forks, B.C.

After arriving at my friend's home, I unpacked and got ready to preach. Before I brought the Word, I mentioned my missing carry-on bag and then went on with the service, not giving it a second thought. We had great meetings; the week flew by too quickly, and it was time to return back home. I boarded my commuter jet and flew to Vancouver, this time arriving early enough in the day to catch a connecting flight back to Seattle. My travel agent had made tight connections; after going through customs, I hurriedly made my way to my airline check-in counter. There were three people in line already, and the woman just in front of me was smoking a cigarette and blowing the smoke away from me, but it still wafted toward me with its nauseating odor. I tried to look in the opposite direction from where she was blowing the smoke while I moved up in line. *Two more people to go.*

Oh, I wish they would hurry, I thought. *I don't want to miss my plane.* Then I looked up at the sign above the agent who was working behind the counter and suddenly realized that I was at the wrong counter! I quickly looked around for the right counter, and then I took a quick glance back at the agent behind the counter. When I looked, *this time* there were two men standing there. Just then, the one who had just arrived looked at me with a glint in his eyes, smiled, and lifted his arm up high. In his hand was my red carry-on bag! I squealed and yelled out, "That's my bag!" The other agent looked at this man, then looked at me, looked back at this "agent" again, and said, "Lady, if you have your tag for it, it's yours." I said very assertively, "I sure do." With that, I opened my purse and produced the tag; he took it from the other man, compared the tag, and exclaimed, "It's yours!"

I grabbed it, said "Thank you," and unzipped the side compartment. Sure enough, there was my velvet case. I could hardly believe my eyes! I quickly opened it up in front of the woman who was taking a long drag of her cigarette, and when I saw my jewelry intact, I said in a very enthusiastic voice, "Oh, praise the Lord!" She chimed in, "Yesssss...." Then I remembered that I had a plane to catch, so I took off running to get to the right counter. As I was running to the counter, the man who had produced my carry-on was walking toward me, and I thought, *I just have to stop and give him a quick testimony.*

As I was slowing down to a fast-paced stride, I approached him and looked into his eyes again, and they were so intense and shiny and unusual. As I went to open my mouth, I heard the Holy Spirit say loudly in my spirit, "He knows!" I thought and agreed, *He knows!*—not really understanding what that meant but not having the time to think about it then. So rather than stop to tell him my story, I kept walking as quickly as I could to board my Seattle-bound flight. When I settled into my assigned seat, I breathing a sigh of relief and thanked the Lord for bringing my jewelry back. *Wonderful, now I will not have to face Mike with the story of my lost jewelry.*

When I got back home, I told my husband the story of finding my jewelry, still not fully realizing what had *really happened* but so grateful for recovering my loss. After sharing the story with Mike, I decided to sit down and write my friend a "Thank you" card; I started out by telling her how much I appreciated her hospitality and then added a post script: "Oh, by the way, an angel..." "*An angel?*" I said aloud. I stopped writing, and then I really squealed, "Mike, that man was an angel who brought my carry-on bag to the airport. Mike, he was an angel!"

Mike looked at me for a long moment with one of those looks and said with a smile, "Oh yeah, sure, Flo" and went back to what he was doing. Mike is the more practical of us and an angel returning my jewelry was, at that time, more than he could believe. I thought, *No one is going to take away my joy*, so I got on the phone and called my friend long distance: "Pastor Sam, you are *not* going to believe what just happened to me..." I went on and told him the story, not leaving out one detail (as only a woman can do), and then I waited for *his* response. He immediately retorted (I could hear a smile in his voice), "Of course it was an angel, Flo! Do you think that *agent* was standing there for a *whole week* waiting for you to return to the airport (at the wrong counter), and that at *precisely* the moment you looked up, he lifted up your carry-on bag so you could see it? Now what do you suppose the mathematical probability of that would be?" With that question in mind, we both laughed. I said, "Sam, he looked like an Italian. He was short and stocky and had black hair. Pastor Sam, an Italian-looking angel brought back my jewelry! Oh, thank you, Jesus."

An Angel Brings His Glasses

I had shared this story with my good friends Mike and Mary (who have now gone on to be with the Lord). Once, when they were fishing in the Chilkat River near Haines, Alaska, Mike's glasses fell into the river. They groaned, because they did not have the money to buy another pair of glasses, so they decided to pray about it. After they prayed, committing it to the Lord, Mary's eyes lit up with revelation, and she shouted, "Mike, remember when Sister Flo told us her angel story? Well, Mike, we can pray and ask the Lord to send an angel to help us." They did, and then they drove to Haines to pick up some supplies. When they returned, Mike's glasses were sitting on top of a rock in the Chilkat River, and they were dripping wet!

Angels Join in the Service

Early in 1993, a pastor invited me to conduct a two night "Holy Ghost and Fire Rally" in Craig, Alaska, at the Pentecostal Church of God. It was the same church where a revival had broken out in the early 1950s, and they saw such supernatural signs as tongues of fire over the church building and oil pouring out of people's hands. Sister Hensyel, who saw those tongues of fire on the building, said that, as they shot up into the air, the flames became angels and ascended into Heaven. (This same scene happened to Manoah in Judges 13:20 when the angel of the Lord ascended in the flame of the altar.) On the first night at this church, where so many signs and wonders had happened in the '50s revival, that same anointing was there once again, touching the people. We all went home refreshed by the presence of the Lord, but what happened the next night was beyond our expectation. The meeting started with loud enthusiastic praise, and the Indian people got up to dance before the Lord. When we hit a high point in the music, I looked over at my 80-year-old uncle, Theodore, and he had his eyes closed, dancing under the anointing of the Lord like a young man, not bumping into anyone. Then I looked over at Judy, thinking about how she played the piano during the '50s revival with the same enthusiasm. I began watching her husband, who was playing the guitar (like Chuck Berry), when all of a sudden, he looked toward his wife with this startled look on his face. He took his guitar off and broke into holy dancing. The entire atmosphere changed. The joy of the Lord spread like fire, and soon everyone was dancing.

As I continued to watch, three young men stopped, turned around, and looked as if they saw something. They stood there for a brief moment, and then all three were thrown to the floor and began laughing in the Spirit. I looked over at a young girl sitting on the front row, and her face was glistening from the glory and red from the fire of God. She was speaking in tongues, so I went over to her to see if she wanted to give a prophetic word. She looked at me to speak, but only tongues came out. She struggled again to say something in English, but she could only speak in tongues.

Then the guitar player came over and told me that, as he was looking at his wife playing the piano, some papers fell off the piano onto the floor, so she bent over to pick them up, but to his surprise (and hers), the piano kept playing! He said that was when he took off his guitar and started dancing with all his might. That angel that played the piano did not miss a note or the beat!

The people lingered until almost midnight, not wanting to go home, but the pastor wanted to close down the meeting because the next day was Palm Sunday. So he went to the pulpit, put on his guitar, and tried to strum it, but no sound came out. He strummed repeatedly but still missed the strings. Then he tried to speak and could not say a word. He stood there speechless, looking dumbfounded, for about five minute. When he could finally speak, he said, "I have never not been able to speak before in my life!"

When the meeting was finally over, I went over to the three young men, and I asked them what happened to them. They told me that when they turned around and looked, there was a cloud that came rolling in from the back of the church; when it came and covered their heads, they were slain in the spirit and rolled and laughed in the joy of the Lord.

The next day, the young woman who could not speak in English testified to all of us that when she went home to her mother she still could not speak in English. When her mother saw the glory and the fire on her face and heard the tongues, she fell to her knees and gave glory to Jesus.

Angel Drives Car

Many years ago, some leaders invited me to the Swan Indian Reservation for revival meetings. I knew the reservation was on I-90, but those were the days before MapQuest, so I did not have exact driving instructions. I do not have any sense of direction, so my husband was rightfully apprehensive over this trip. I was not sure how I was going to get there, but I was confident in the Lord who lives in me. I left with joy in my heart, thinking about all the wonderful new Indian leaders I was going to meet. It was getting dark, and I was starting to get a little uneasy about driving in the dark because I was having difficulty seeing the highway signs at night. When I get into situations like this, I start to pray in my heavenly language. I prayed and drove, but I did not see any signs leading to the reservation. I prayed more when, all of a sudden, I felt the wheel of my car turn sharply to the right, and there was the sign to the reservation! The angel who accompanies me took control of the wheel because he saw that I was about to drive right past that reservation. Where I would have ended up that night, I do not know. Angels are with us to help us accomplish the will of God in the earth.

These are holy days—the last days—when God's glory will be seen everywhere, when the average saint will do the greater works Jesus spoke about in the Gospels. The Lord is bringing to the forefront men and women who fear only God and who will shake the earth with apostolic preaching and mighty demonstrations of the Spirit. Ministers filled with the fiery boldness of Jesus will grab cancers and say "in the name of Jesus," and the cancers will release their grip. Angelic beings will come from the throne room, bringing deliverance to some, messages to a few, impartations to others, and maybe even returning your jewelry or your glasses. These are days of the miraculous, of supernatural beings, and of great signs and wonders so that the world might know that Jesus is alive!

Chapter 9

DEMONIC SPIRITS

A demon, sent to kill me, interrupted my joy-filled days shortly after my salvation experience in early 1971. It was a dark, lonely night when a demonic force entered my bedroom through the ceiling. My husband Mike was working a late shift, and our four daughters were tucked in bed in the back bedroom. I was lying on our bed with our little Maltese dog "Izzie" beside me; Both of us were fully relaxed and trailing off to sleep when I began to sense a cold, sinister force. I stared into the dark, trying to see what it was, when Izzie made a muffled sound, jumped off the bed, and hid under the box springs. As I lay hardly breathing, I sensed this ominous being come over me, causing me great trepidation—it paralyzed me. Then this foreboding being began to descend from the ceiling down over me, permeating the room with its presence. Terrified and frozen with fear, I tried to open my mouth to scream, but I could not even move. Then courage rose up in me, and I heard in my mind these words, *JESUS, JESUS, JESUS!*

> I know demons cannot understand our thoughts, but God can. He heard my plea for help, and He sent me deliverance. As slowly as this force came down on me, it slowly started to lift in submission and then fled from the room. I thanked the Lord and breathed a sigh of relief as the beads of perspiration began to roll down my face.

The next day, I went to see my pastor, but he could not give me an explanation for the appearance of this demonic entity or the power it had over me. I thought my days of dealing with demonic powers were over now that I knew Jesus as my Lord and Savior, but it was just the beginning of my education in spiritual warfare. As a child, I knew of these dark powers in the Indian village where I grew up. These demons use to torment us by knocking on our windows at night; dogs would begin to howl exactly at midnight, and witches and warlocks would turn into animals—some flying through the air. Nevertheless, my battle against the forces of wickedness was *not* over.

> However, before Jesus could teach me about these powers, and how to do deliverance on others tormented by forces from hell, He first had to deliver me.

LIVING IN THE MORTUARY

A few short years after I had given my heart to Jesus, Mike and I had an opportunity to live close to our pastor, who we loved, and to supplement our income so that we could save to purchase our own home. Our church had seen great increase during its revival, and the once adequate building was now too small to accommodate our growing congregation, so the elders voted to purchase the building across from our church. It was the local mortuary. After we bought the building, our pastor and the church board made plans to build an apartment on the upper level and to put in a bookstore and coffee house ministry for troubled youth on the lower level.

When Mike and I heard that they were looking for part-time janitors for the church and caretakers for the newly-acquired ministry building, we applied for the position and got it. We packed up our meager belongings, and we moved into the mortuary, trying to ignore the stale odor of cigarettes, the smoke-stained walls, and the discarded clothing that lay in a heap near the embalming fluids. (These items were later thrown away.) As we examined every room and elevator, Mike noticed that each room had a buzzer on the wall that was wired to the main living room. When we saw the black streaks of cigarette stains, which had run down the walls from chain smokers, and the buzzers in every room, we could sense that the previous owners had obviously lived in dread and terror—but of what?

After living in our new apartment for only a few weeks, I noticed that I was becoming increasingly short tempered and that our daughters more unruly. One night, Mike came home from work, and while we sat in silence at the dinner table, without warning, he covered his face with his hands and started sobbing. I tried to console him and queried why he was crying, but he would not answer me. What was happening in my home? What was happening to my family?

One day, after I had gotten off work (I worked for our state legislature), I came home and found Mike just sitting in the living room. When I walked through the door, he did not give me his usual greeting with a kiss but began to tell me about two eerie instances that had just happened. He said that when he came home, as he was brewing some coffee in the kitchen, he heard the washer going. Thinking I was home, he went to the washer/dryer area, but to his amazement, the washer was agitating without any clothes or water in it. He thought that was odd, but he dismissed it and went to the basement where he began to work on his car, which he had driven in through the double doors. Our dog was sitting by his side, watching him work. Then from the corner of his eye, he thought he saw something black go by, so he looked, and there it was again—*something* whooshed past him. It was large and dark and left him with a cold chill. Then our dog made a quick dash, running up the stairs as fast as his little legs would carry him. Mike called to the dog, but he refused to come back down. Mike felt a cold draft go down his spine, so he quickly left the basement.

After telling me that story, he told me to call my Christian friends to come to this house—this mortuary—and do some spiritual house cleaning. I immediately called those I knew who understood the spiritual realm, and they all agreed to come at the designated time to pray throughout the building.

When they arrived, they started at the bottom and worked their way up to the third level, praying in tongues and asking the Lord to show them what needed to be expelled.

When they finished the Lord's work, we all rejoiced in His goodness and His power. We thought the job completed until a few weeks later when the nightmare took on a new twist.

Mike was at work and the girls were visiting their friends, so I thought I would take advantage of the peace and quiet and take a nap. As I lay there trying to doze off, I felt strangely agitated inside. Then my stomach started to churn, and I thought I must have eaten the wrong thing. Again, I tried to relax when my lower abdomen started to move, twist, and turn. I looked down at my stomach; I was startled when my belly began to extend as if I was seven months pregnant. As I was watching, it looked as if a huge snake was inside of me! My belly was moving up and down and sideways and did not stop until I screamed out in stark terror! I jumped up off the bed and called my friend Ramona. I told her what was happening, and she said to drive up to her house right away. As soon as I hung up, she called another close friend Kathy for added prayer support. When I arrived, they were both waiting for me. They took me right into the living room, and we all got down on our knees and starting praying. As I listened to them pray, hatred welled up in me as I had never experienced before, and my precious friend Kathy was the recipient of that hate. I loathed her and felt like striking out at her, but I did not know why. *What is happening to me?* As they continued to pray, I became rigid—unaffected by their fervent prayers.

Ramona must have seen the hatred in my eyes, because she rose up suddenly from her kneeling position, grabbed my head with both hands, and with all authority commanded that *thing* to let go and come out of me. As the battle went on, she would not take her trembling hands off my head, despite my resistance. Suddenly, my body re-laxed, and then I felt total peace as I was set free in Jesus' name!

JESUS' DELIVERANCE MINISTRY

Jesus spent one-third of His ministry casting out demons, and He taught His disciples to continue with this ministry: *"As you go, preach, saying, 'The kingdom of heaven is at hand.' Heal the sick, cleanse the lepers, raise the dead, cast out demons."* (Matt. 10:7-8). In some Christian circles, we have no problem laying hands on the sick for healing, but we refuse to cast out devils. For instance, some cancers are caused by a demon and need to be cast out; *we then* pray for a healing where that cancer did physical damage.

If we cast demons out of a person who is not saved, Jesus said in Matthew 12:45, *"…the last state of that man is worse than the first."* We either need to get them born again and then cast out the demons, or we need to cast out the demons and then get them born again.

When we are born again, our spirit is transformed from dark-ness to light, and we are liberated from the dominion of darkness (see Col. 1:13). The Word tells us that Jesus *"raised us up together, and made us sit together in the heavenly places in Christ Jesus"* (Eph. 2:6). That is true "positionally" but not experientially. We need to walk some things out. Ephesians 2:8 says, *"For by grace you have been saved through faith."* That is past tense. At conversion, our spirits are saved, but our minds and bodies are not. Romans 12:1-2 states, *"I beseech you therefore, brethren, by the mercies of God, that you present your bodies a living sacrifice, holy, acceptable to God, which is your reasonable service. And do not be conformed to this world, but be transformed by the renewing of your mind."*

When Jesus comes, First Thessalonians 4:16-17 declares that *"the Lord Himself will descend from heaven with a shout, with the voice of an archangel, and with the trumpet of God. And the **dead** in Christ will rise first. Then we who are alive and remain shall be caught up together with them...."*

> Therefore, our spirits *were saved*; our minds are *being saved*; and our bodies *will be saved*.

When a person is born again, they bring some baggage with them from their past. That is why doctors ask you to fill out a medical questionnaire that asks if either of your parents had a particular disease, because if your momma had cancer or your father had heart disease, you may have inherited that disease. If you were involved in the occult or secret societies, you may have brought demonic forces with you when you were saved, and if the church you attend does not believe in deliverance after salvation, you may well suffer (in your soul) until delivered. Some new believers are delivered by just simply loving on Jesus and devouring the Word; some need hands-on deliverance; others need to renounce sins, and then, in the privacy of their own homes, they will be delivered by the Lord Himself. If you participate in your own deliverance or assist in helping another person to be set free, never fear the demon, because Jesus, the Holy Spirit, and the angels are with you to help you.

TWELVE BASKETS FULL

During the three-and-a-half decades that I have served the Lord, I have encountered demonic forces, but with each encounter, the Holy Spirit has taught me how to deal more effectively with these wicked forces. In my early years, at times, I felt inadequate or helpless, but the Lord was always faithful to remind me that the greater One lives in me. In one of those teaching sessions, He led me to the "12 baskets full" story that is in all four Gospels. In this story, He showed me not to fear the enemy but to always trust in Him because of His abiding presence.

Mark 6:30-52 gives the best narration of this story. It begins with the disciples coming to Jesus, giving a detailed account of their ministry and the things they taught the people. Jesus could see they were exhausted from the work, so He told them to "*Come aside by yourselves to a deserted place and rest a while*" (Mark 6:31).

> Not recognizing exhaustion has caused many ministers to make mistakes or to yield to temptation, shipwrecking their faith.

Jesus knew that, so He provided a time of rest and relaxation for them. However, the multitude saw them leaving and knew where they were going, so they ran on foot and arrived before the disciples and Jesus landed on shore. When Jesus saw how great the multitude was, He was moved with compassion, and He began to teach them many things. When evening came, the disciples came to Jesus and said, "*This is a deserted place and the hour is late*" (Mark 6:35).

> They were saying, Jesus, this is a hard, dark place…but it is never too hard or too dark for Jesus to work, regardless of what the situation is or where you live.

The disciples' strength still had not returned, so they told Jesus to send the people away to the next village to find food, but Jesus made an astounding remark to his disciples: "*You give them something to eat*" (Mark 6:37). The disciples might have thought, **We** *have to give them something to eat! We thought* **You** *were the miracle-worker. Besides, it is too far to the next village; we are tired, and we do not have any money to buy this crowd any food.* Jesus did not listen to their weak excuses.

He said to them, "*How many loaves do you have?*" The lesson begins. They said, "*Five, and two fish.*" How could this small amount feed such a mass of people? Jesus commanded the people to sit down on the green grass in ranks of 100 and 50, and He took the five loaves and two fish and "*...looked up to heaven, blessed and broke the loaves and gave them to His disciples to set before them*" (Mark 6:38-41). What happened here? Jesus broke the loaves and gave some to Peter, then some to Andrew, to James, John, Philip, Bartholomew, Thomas, Matthew the publican, James the son of Alphaeus, Thaddaeus, Simon the Canaanite, and Judas Iscariot (who later betrayed Him). As He put the broken bread in their hands, they turned and gave it to the multitude. The creative miracle came from Jesus, but it was multiplying in *their* hands.

With this story, Jesus was teaching them what He was about to do with their lives. He would first bless them and teach them, and then He would "break" their stubbornness so that He could use them to touch the world with His creative power.

He showed them how creative miracles come—through prayer. Some think Jesus did this miracle by Himself. No, He did not. He did the miracle by the same Holy Spirit He wants you to rely upon. Jesus did His creative works by the anointing of the Holy Spirit, not by His divine attributes. Second Peter 1:4 says, "*Whereby are given unto us exceeding great and precious promises; that by these* [the promises] *ye might be partakers of the divine nature…*" (KJV).

Remember when Jesus came to earth as a babe, the anointing did not come upon Him until He was by the River Jordan. The Holy Spirit descended in the form of a dove, and it landed on Him and remained upon Him throughout His ministry on earth (see Luke 3:21-22). Jesus was showing us that we must also depend solely upon the Holy Spirit, and as we yield to Him, He (the Holy Spirit) will do the *greater works* that Jesus spoke of.

The Bible says that we have received this power. What is this power?

It is the powerful person of the Holy Spirit who lives in us; that is, if we are born again. Jesus' command in Acts 1:4-8 makes this very clear: "*And being assembled together with them, He commanded them not to depart from Jerusalem, but to wait for the Promise of the Father…'you shall receive power when the Holy Spirit has come upon you….'*"

These creative miracles did not happen just in the New Testament under Jesus' ministry. The gift of miracles occurred in the Old Testament as well. Elisha operated in this gift when he multiplied the 20 loaves of bread to feed the 100 men in Second Kings 4:42-44.

BACK TO THE STORY

When the disciples and Jesus fed the multitude, the Bible says they did not stop until the people ate *"as much as they wanted"* (John 6:11). If you hunger for more of Jesus, He will always completely satisfy your soul and spirit like no one else can.

The Bible says that after the people were contented, Jesus sent them home, and the disciples picked up 12 baskets full of the fragments. Then He *"made His disciples get into the boat and go before Him to the other side,"* but Jesus went to the mountain to pray (Mark 6:45-46).

When you finish a great meeting, follow Jesus' example: go and pray lest the enemy take undue advantage of you in your weakened condition.

When the evening came, the boat was in the middle of the sea; a dreadful storm arose, and the *"wind was against them"* (Mark 6:48). Jesus, from His vantage point, saw them straining at rowing, getting nowhere, so He left His place of prayer and came to them, walking on the water. They thought He was a ghost and were screaming in terror when He said to them, *"Take heart! I AM! Stop being alarmed and afraid"* (Mark 6:50b AMP). When He stepped into their boat, the wind stopped howling, and they were astonished beyond measure. Then it tells us a very important fact: *"For they had not understood about the loaves, because their heart was hardened"* (Mark 6:52). What was there to understand? In the midst of that stormy trial, they forgot how the creative miracle multiplied in their own hands.

As a reminder, they *each* had a basket *full* of the miracle food, and it was in the boat with them.

Jesus was showing them that He would not always be with them, but the miracle-working power (the Holy Spirit) was there with them whenever they had need.

There was no reason for them to fear, because even on that mountain (and now in Heaven), Jesus saw what they were going through, and He would not let them perish; He had a plan for their lives: *"Immediately He made His disciples get into the boat and go before Him to the other side...."*

If He tells you to go on that mission trip, get on that plane, help with deliverance, or go to the other side, you can be assured of success, because He will be with you as you go. There is no need to be overly concerned when you have *your* "basket" (evidence of His power) in your boat (symbolic of your ministry), for He is with you and watching over you. In First John 2:27, it says, *"But as for you, the anointing (the sacred appointment, the unction) which you received from Him abides [permanently] in you..."* (AMP).

Paul also writes:

And do not [for a moment] be frightened or intimidated in anything by your opponents and adversaries, for such [constancy and fearlessness] will be a clear sign (proof and seal) to them of [their impending] destruction, but [a sure token and evidence] of your deliverance and salvation, and that from God (Philippians 1:28 AMP).

WOMAN TRIES TO RIP HER THROAT OUT

Many years after the experience in that awful mortuary, the Lord started sending me to the nations of the world. There was one country I enjoyed going to because of the miraculous power I witnessed there. Almost every time I went there, I did some form of deliverance. It became apparent to me, and to the pastor I worked with, that the Lord was teaching me specifics about spiritual warfare. Each time I went to that nation, a woman named Magda (not her real name) needed special attention. Magda's father, who belonged to a coven, had dedicated her to satan when she was three weeks old. As she grew up, she became a "sacrifice" to satan, and the warlocks continually raped her on the altar. When that happened, she had learned to make her spirit leave her body (astral travel) until they finished raping her so that she would not feel any pain. It was during a Halloween weekend that my pastor friend Pastor David (not his real name) led her in the sinner's prayer, and she gave her life to the Lord Jesus.

When the members of the coven heard about her Halloween night conversion, they were enraged and tried to have her killed. (Halloween is their big night to be involved in the most bizarre activity.) They attacked her in the spirit, and Pastor David had his hands full trying to keep her alive. Just before I flew to this country to conduct a series of revival meetings, Magda ended up in the hospital with a mysterious illness. In this hospital, there were witches and warlocks who were some of the doctors and nurses, and these servants of satan attempted to kill her. When Pastor David went to visit her, she told him that someone had sewn a hormone patch on her lower abdomen. When Pastor David looked at it, he knew by the Spirit that this was not a hormone patch, so he laid his hands on her, and it disappeared. This infuriated these servants from hell, so they put another "patch" on her; again Pastor David laid hands on that area, and again it disappeared, this time scar and all!

Just before Magda was discharged from this hospital, a nurse inserted a catheter in her bladder and then removed it, leaving a crystal inside of her. They used this as a point of contact to touch her body to destroy her. When I had arrived in this country, I went to my host's home and prepared for my meetings. I went to the first meeting, and toward the end of the meeting, Magda slipped in and sat in the back row. Slightly slumped over, Magda would look at me, and instead of smiling at me as she always had, she looked lifeless, depressed, and ashen.

After my teaching, I went over to her and put my arms around her, but she pulled away with a pained expression on her face. I asked her what was wrong, and as she sat erect, I was amazed to see that her belly was the size of an eight-month pregnant woman. I asked her again what was wrong with her, and she told me that she had not urinated in eight days! My mother's heart reached out to her, and I laid my hands on her and began to pray for her healing. As I did that, she moaned in pain, jerked away from me, and ran out the back door. (Later, after her deliverance, she told me the moment I laid hands on her, the spirit that was in her belly caused her much pain, causing her to flee.)

I found Pastor David and asked him in a somewhat demanding tone what had happened to her and why he had not done anything about her condition. He told me that he knew she had not urinated in eight days, but the Lord had told him to wait until I arrived to pray with him for her deliverance. *Deliverance!* I thought. *No wonder she squirmed away from me.* Always check in with the Holy Spirit as you minister; the real need may not be a healing, but a deliverance. Pastor David told me that after the evening service we would pray for her. He then instructed me to preach that night; when I gave the altar call, if she came up for prayer, I was to lay hands on her. All that day, I stayed in my prayer closet seeking the Lord for the evening meeting.

The meeting started, and Magda came walking through the door and sat toward the back of the church. I was glad she had come. When I preached and gave the altar call, Magda came forward. She was slain by the power of God, and when she got up, she had regressed to speaking and acting like an 8-year-old child, asking for Pastor David. I was very perplexed over her child-like behavior and speech.

Pastor David came to me and called his mother (who was a worker in the church) to help. He said, "Mother, you will pray in tongues, and Flo, you will plead the blood of the Lamb, and I will do the deliverance." We agreed, took Magda by the hand, and led her to the pastor's office. After Magda sat down on the recliner, Pastor David got up and locked the office door. I thought with a slight panic, *What is he doing, and why is he locking us in?* He is very perceptive and looked at me as if to answer my unspoken question. "It is to keep her from leaving." Oh good, I thought. At least it is not to keep *me* in. His mother began to pray in tongues. I began to plead the blood as instructed. Pastor David got down on his knees in front of her, so I got down on the floor too.

Pastor David started praying in the spirit, and I could tell he was waiting for the Lord to give him his first instruction. All of a sudden, he blew on her, and she was slain in the spirit! I looked at him with suspicion, wondering what he had done, and he explained, "That is what the witches and hypnotists do, but it is a counterfeit." He said he did it so that she would not remember what happened and could maintain her dignity. *How kind,* I thought. Pastor David continued with the deliverance and gave me instructions on how to assist him. I did as commanded.

I kept my eyes open all the time, watching Magda for any sudden attack from the enemy through her. Then I looked at her huge belly and remembered it was full of urine! I looked down at my favorite white dress and looked back at her belly; I looked at my dress, then looked at her belly. I thought, *Oh dear Jesus, we are going to pray for her, and when we do, she is going to blow that urine all over my favorite dress and me!* Just then, I saw her eyeballs darting wildly under her eyelids. David said, "The devil is giving her bad dreams." He commanded the bad dreams and visions to stop. As he finished that prayer, she began to lift her strong arms in the air, and her hands slowly curled up in a claw-like position.

David yelled, "Flo, hold her arms down, she is going to try and rip her throat out!" *I thought, rip her throat out! RIP her throat out! Oh great, this is going to hit the front page of the local newspaper: "Evangelist From Alaska Kills Woman in Church Office."* I grabbed her arms, and my hands felt like vise-grips as the Holy Spirit strengthened my hold on her. Amazingly, she could not get away from my grip. The Holy Spirit had to help me, because she was at least nine inches taller than I am and about 75 pounds heavier.

David's mother intensified the tongues, and I kept pleading the blood of Jesus over her and us. David then commanded me to lay my hands on her belly. I did, and he put his hand over my hands, took authority over that demon, and asked the angels to burn it out. Then he commanded that evil spirit to come out in Jesus' name! He prayed once again, but this time he asked Jesus to absorb all that fluid in her stomach. The moment he did, her huge belly instantaneously deflated right in front of my eyes! I sat there, totally awestruck at the mighty God we serve! He blew on her a second time, called her by name, and commanded her to come back. She opened her eyes and asked for a cup of coffee, not knowing what had just happened to her. Her dignity was intact, and we left the office rejoicing in Jesus' great delivering power!

HOW TO WALK IN VICTORY

Most of us had issues in our lives when we were born again. Once they are dealt with, either through healing and/or deliverance, we must learn how to stay clean, stay delivered, and maintain the freedom that Jesus brought to us.

Romans 6 presents us with a number of keys for learning to walk in victory and *"newness of life"*:

> *Therefore we were buried with Him through baptism into death, that just as Christ was raised from the dead by the glory of the Father, even so we also should walk in newness of life. For if we have been united together in the likeness of*

His death, certainly we also shall be in the likeness of His resurrection, knowing this, that our old man was crucified with Him, that the body of sin might be done away with, that we should no longer be slaves of sin (Romans 6:4-6).

The only way the *"old man"* (our old adamic nature, which was our nature before we were born again) can be dealt with is through the cross of Jesus Christ, and we need to "crucify" the old man daily.

Likewise you also, reckon [consider] yourselves to be dead indeed to sin, but alive to God in Christ Jesus our Lord. Therefore, do not let sin reign in your mortal body, that you should obey it in its lusts. And do not present your members as instruments of unrighteousness to sin, but present yourselves to God as being alive from the dead, and your members as instruments of righteousness to God. For sin shall not have dominion over you... (Romans 6:11-14).

Our spiritual perception, particularly what we "consider" to be true about ourselves, is a key element to walking in victory. Paul, in these passages, is admonishing the Romans to "consider" themselves rightly and to take action accordingly. If you are going to walk in victory, you must determine to:

+ Reckon or consider yourself to be dead to sin

+ Present yourself alive unto God in unbroken fellowship with Him

+ Read and study the Word, applying what you have learned

+ Walk in newness of life, habitually living and behaving in a new way

+ Begin to develop new habits by suppressing the old ones

+ Become a servant or love slave of God through radical praise

+ Worship and adore Him, for as you do, you are set free

Remember the promise of a divine exchange in Isaiah 61:3: *"To appoint unto them that mourn in Zion, to give them beauty for ashes, the oil of joy for mourning, the **garment of praise** for the **spirit of heaviness…"** (KJV).

THE LAST DAYS' HARVEST

We are the 40th Jubilee generation since Jesus walked this earth. We are the mature sons and daughters of God, stripped of our pride and our own ways, so that Jesus might live in and through us. We have been to Heaven's gate, and we have *"tasted the good word of God and the powers of the age to come"* (Hebrews 6:5) for one purpose and one purpose alone: to touch the Magda's of this world. We fully understand the original fivefold mandate to *"be fruitful and multiply…"* (Gen. 1:27-28).

We are not "of this world," and we march to the sound of a different Drummer. The huge responsibility that we have been entrusted with is to bring in the lost and dying—the Magda's of our generation. Jesus said, *"…the harvest is the end of the age…"* (Matt. 13:39), and we have now come to that time; therefore, let it be said of us, as it was said of Mordecai in Esther 10:3, that we are *"seeking the good of* [our] *people and speaking peace to* [our] *whole race."*

Chapter 10

SPIRITUAL REVOLUTIONARIES

Revival is renewed conviction of sin and repentance, followed by an intense desire to live in obedience to God. It is giving up one's will to God in deep humility.

—Charles Finney[1]

ARE YOU WILLING TO DIE FOR JESUS?

"Are *you* willing to die for Jesus and the for sake of the Gospel?" my teacher belted out! All my instructors at Gerald Derstine's Bible school were wonderful, but we had this one who was a very strict, unambiguous prophet/teacher who I respected very much. I do not think he was the students' favorite, but I liked his in-your-face, can't-get-way-with-anything style. He had been teaching from Mark 8:34-38, where Jesus had called the people

233

and His disciples to Himself and said to them, *"Whoever desires to come after Me, let him deny himself, and take up his cross and follow Me. For whoever loses his life for My sake and the gospel's will save it."*

"Are *you* willing to die for Jesus and for the sake of the Gospel?" When those words came out of his mouth, it struck my spirit so hard that hot, stinging tears welled up in my eyes, and I did not hear another word he said during that class. I sat there completely undone by the Lord, unable to move, all the while shouting in my spirit, *Will you please hurry and get this class over with!* Finally, he dismissed us. I bolted out of my seat, ran out of the building into the warm sun, found my spot by the duck pond, and began to weep profusely, unashamedly, as that question rang through my mind repeatedly: *Are you willing to die for Jesus and for the sake of the Gospel?*

When God asks you a question like that, you cannot answer Him quickly, mindlessly, or carelessly—for He will take you at your word. I prayed and contemplated the price that I would have to pay to live fully for Him. Some Christian teachers tell us that we do not have to pay a price because Jesus already paid the price. Oh really? He *did* pay the ultimate price, but He requires something of us if we want to go beyond the superficial and go deep in Him. This kind of Christianity is not for the fickle or capricious.

"Let him deny himself…" *What you are asking of me, Jesus, is hard, very hard. You are infringing on my rights. Are you suggesting that I can no longer rely on my own self-dependence? All right, I will*

give up all my own self-interests, even my self-pursuits, and I will follow You. He was not satisfied. The probing went deeper.

"*Take up his cross.*" This is not Jesus' cross, but *my* cross— where my will and His will cross. *This is infinitely more difficult, Lord,* I continued to whine. *You know I have a very strong will, Lord.* Somehow, I sensed He was not listening to my protests and carnal reasoning. However, I was honest with Him. *I want to do it my way, Lord—but I will follow You all the way; all right, I will concede to Your will and acquiesce to Your desires.*

"*And follow Me.*" *If I promise to follow You, where will you take me?* Jesus answered me, speaking ever so softly, "Follow Me."

"*For whoever loses his life for My sake and the Gospel's will save it.*" *How can I deny You, Lord? How can I say no when You have done so much for me?* I sensed that my inner struggle was almost over. *I will totally consecrate my life to Him,* I thought, with tears streaming down my face. *Whatever Jesus wants from me, He can take and use for His glory.* After three hours of deep introspection, my spirit yielded up to the only One who ever really loved me, to the One who gave His life for me so that I might live.

> Now I was giving up my life to Him, *so that He could live in me.* Paul the apostle said in Galatians 2:20, "*I have been crucified with Christ; it is no longer I who live, but Christ lives in me; and the life which I now live in the flesh I live by faith in the Son of God, who loved me and gave Himself for me.*"

"OK, Lord," I said in my own dramatic way, "OK, I will give my life for You, Jesus, and for the sake of Your Gospel!" I waited for

Heaven to roll with a clap of thunder in approval, but there was not even a flash of lightening—only silence.

> Then Jesus whispered in my heart, "Now you are ready to live for Me, Flo; for you were not ready to live for Me *until* you were willing to die for Me."

After that encounter with the Lord, things seemed fresher, lighter—until the Lord began to go deeper in my soul and spirit. The probing was not over yet. Several years before I had attended the Institute of Ministry in Bradenton, Florida, the Holy Spirit spoke through a sister and gave me Isaiah 54:6-14. I mused over that portion of Scripture many times after it was given to me, "*For the Lord has called you like a woman forsaken and grieved in spirit; like a youthful wife when you were refused...O you afflicted one, tossed with tempest, and not comforted...in righteousness you shall be established....*" Those verses were very descriptive of my life, but because of Jesus, my quality of living dramatically changed and life was good, very good.

Several weeks after I had that "duck pond" experience with the Lord, He led me to another season of prayer. Bible school was almost over, and I was anticipating a special time of reunion with my precious husband Mike. As I was on my daily walk after our classes were over for the day, the Holy Spirit told me that I was to spend another hour in prayer, but I was to go to a secluded place atop the dorm where I lived. I immediately went there and began to pace slowly around the roof praying in the spirit; then the examining began. He asked me if I was truly willing to give up *everything* for the sake of the Gospel and for Jesus Christ. I told Him I was, but I could tell that He was not persuaded with my answer—it was too glib. Again, He pressed me for a response. I knew He was going for something I had missed—something I forgot to include in the "everything" I had previously given to Him.

Then He asked, "Are you willing to give up your 'Isaac'?"

My "Isaac"? "Who is my 'Isaac,' Lord?"

The Lord said, "Your husband Mike."

"NO, LORD, NO! I cannot do that. I cannot give him up. No, I won't do it!"

The Lord responded, "I thought you said you would give up everything for the sake of My Gospel." My pace was quicker now as I walked around and around that rooftop struggling with this decision. I just *knew* that, if I said "yes" to the Holy Spirit, He would take the one on this earth that I loved more than anything, more than anyone else. Mike was the one person I cherished above all. The Lord was right; he *was* my "Isaac."

"No Lord," I moaned as my voice trailed away, expressing the agony within. Then the Holy Spirit got ever so quiet and waited patiently for my final answer. The air seemed thick with His presence. The birds seemed to stand still waiting for His next move—and my answer. My strength now gone, the battle was over. In submission, I yielded up my "Isaac" to him. I whispered meekly a simple "yes" to Him.

Then He spoke tenderly to me, "Go to your room and read the rest of Isaiah. I stumbled to my room and opened my Bible. I had read verses six through the end of the chapter many times over;

now He wanted me to read verses 1-5. *"Sing, O barren...*[Lord, I think I can do that] *enlarge the place of your tent...lengthen your cords...*[Sounds good, sounds like He is going to expand me] *do not fear...for you will forget the shame of your youth...*[Thank the Lord, my past is gone forever.] *And you will not remember the reproach of your widowhood* [My widowhood! My widowhood?] *for your Maker is your husband...."* Now I was convinced; the Lord *was* going to take my husband!

"O God," I cried out again; then a peace came sweeping over me. "I give him to you, Lord. He is all yours." I wonder, have I have finally surrendered my all to Him. Though the Lord has not taken my husband from me, He taught me to hold on to him with an attitude of surrender. All that I have and love is the Lord's.

THE IMPERISHABLE CROWN

*Do you not know that those who run in a race all run, but one receives the prize? Run in such a way that you may obtain it. And everyone who competes for the prize is temperate in all things. Now they do it to obtain a perishable crown, but we for an **imperishable crown** (1 Corinthians 9:24-25).*

This imperishable crown or prize is for those who do not consider the sufferings of life to be of any consequence so that they might endure to the end and receive a reward.

BUFFET YOUR BODY

After graduating from Bible School, I traveled throughout southeast Alaska for several years, singing with great gusto and testifying about God's miraculous power. At the conclusion of a particular meeting in Haines, Alaska, an elderly woman with snowy white hair and skin so beautiful it was translucent, allowing the glory within to shine through, came up in line to speak with me. As I listened to her, I wondered who she was. I had not seen her in the meeting, but the way she carried herself made me think she was someone very special to the Lord. She spoke in a quiet tone briefly and slipped a piece of paper in my hand.

When I got back to where I was staying, I pulled the paper out of my pocket, unfolded it, and read these words, "1 Corinthians 9:27." I had my Amplified Bible, so I quickly opened it to read what the Lord was saying to me (thinking it was something great about my ministry or something very uplifting.) It read, *"But [like a boxer] I buffet my body [handle it roughly, discipline it by hardships] and subdue it, for fear that after proclaiming to others the Gospel and things pertaining to it, I myself should become unfit [not stand the test, be unapproved and rejected as a counterfeit]."* When I read those words, my heart sank; then after a long moment, I made a promise to myself to keep my bodily desires and attitudes under control. From that moment, the battle was stronger than ever to destroy my body with physical appetites (and mental challenges), but with the Lord's help, those uncontrollable urges and fiery passions were finally subdued—but not until I had learned how to yield myself totally to the Lord's loving care through prayer and worship. Like a boxer, I have learned how to buffet my body; but it was not easy. Whatever He requires me to give up in denial of self is worth it to win Christ, and in the end, there is an eternal reward (that imperishable crown) in the world to come. After that decision, my life and meetings went to a higher level, and my life filled with a joy and contentment that I had never experienced before.

THE CROWN OF LIFE

Being in full-time ministry or staying an on-fire Christian is not always easy. I recall, when I told my pastor, Pastor McNeven, that the Lord had called me into the ministry, he said, "Always remember this Flo, 'Develop the skin of a rhinoceros and maintain the heart of a Lamb.'" I found out later in my ministry how you develop the skin of a rhinoceros—it is from the scars of many battles! Battles of rejection, battles of misunderstanding, and battles of many kinds, but as I would submit to His tender touch, the anger and frustrations would melt away in His love, keeping my heart tender as a lamb. *"Blessed is the man who endures temptation [trials]; for when He has been approved; he will receive the **crown of life** which the Lord has promised to those who love Him"* (James 1:12).

FIRE FALLS AMONG FIRST NATIONS

The crown of life is given to those who persevere despite hardships, trials, toubles, and every opposition. Preparing for ministry has always had its share of problems, whether they are lack of finances or family crises or other stressful situations. Preparing for a weekend of revival meetings, in 1993, in Canada, among the First Nations people group, was no exception. The only relief from those stressful situations came through much prayer.

On November 3, 1993, at 9:30 P.M., while struggling in prayer for my upcoming meetings, the Lord gave me this word concerning the Native American Indians: "It is truly the time of visitation for the First Nations people," said the Lord. "A downcast people of darkness shall see a great Light; they shall be delivered. Many will rise up in the final moments of this dispensation, and they will be end time leaders who will not parrot words but speak with great clarity, and many shall run to them to hear the Word of the Lord for the hour. It shall be a sound so clear that even as a soprano's voice shatters a glass, so shall My servants shatter many nations to pieces," said the Lord. "Moreover, there shall come a great healing in the land as the wounds of My people are cleansed by the spirit of forgiveness. Then you shall see the "mighty warriors" stand as deliverers, and the cry of the abused shall cease; the alcoholic will drop his bottle; hope will return, and the spirit of suicide will depart as the breach between the races is repaired, for this is surely the hour of My visitation on the Indian Nation," said the Lord.

Immediately after I received that word from the Lord, I got an invitation to fly to Quebec in February to minister among the tribal groups in the surrounding area. In light of that prophecy, I flew into that city with great anticipation. I went to the conference meeting room, and already a large crowd of Canadian First Nations leaders had gathered. After the introduction, I walked to the platform and brought the Word of God with boldness. During the altar call, many of them were slain in the Spirit, and when they could finally get up, they were so *Acts 2 spiritually drunk* in the Lord that they could barely walk. After the meeting, we piled into several vehicles and drove to the nearest restaurant to get a bite to eat.

When I stepped outside the vehicle, the bitter cold hit my face, and I inhaled the minus-degree temperature, hurting my lungs, but the Canadians barely noticed the frigid weather as they filed out of the vehicles in the direction of the restaurant. When the waiters saw us "drunken Indians" coming through the door, they began to whisper to the other staff, who were gawking at us while putting on more pots of coffee. When our food arrived, we could hardly stop laughing to eat. I looked at the oldest man sitting at our table (a church elder) and asked him to bless our food. This man had been sitting with us with a slight look of irritation on his face as we laughed, especially when there was not anything particularly funny. He bowed his head in reverence, and then he said, "O God…" That is as far as he got in his prayer. He sat there stupefied, with his head bowed, unable to lift his head back up so he could eat. We dug into our chicken, and one woman picked up a piece and tried to put her fork in her mouth; her hand got stuck about 10 inches from her face, and I do not know if she ever got that piece of chicken in her mouth. The more we laughed, the more the waiters poured the coffee in our cups, but to their chagrin, we never "sobered" up.

The meetings went on for four nights, and the glory continued to saturate the building as night after night the Lord was touching and changing His people. On one of those nights, Chief Gilliam (not his real name), one of the Grand Chiefs, came up to my product table to purchase some of my singing cassettes and messages. With his big hand, he grabbed three cassettes and gave me a $20 Canadian bill. I reached into my changer to give him $5 in change when he waved with his hand, motioning to me to keep the change. As he waved his hand at me, I was thrown to the floor by the power of God! When I could finally peer over the tabletop and look at him, he was grinning at me. Looking at his hand, and shaking it, he said with a twinkle in his eyes, "Boy, that's hot!" I pulled myself up, we stood there and laughed, and laughed some more as the *"joy unspeakable and full of glory"* filled our souls. All that Jesus-joy more than compensated for the many trials I went through to get to these Quebec meetings.

THE CROWN OF GLORY

Shepherd the flock of God which is among you, serving as overseers, not by compulsion but willingly, not for dishonest *gain but eagerly; nor as being lords over those entrusted to you, but being examples to the flock; and when the Chief Shepherd appears, you will receive the **crown of glory** that does not fade away* (1 Peter 5:2-4).

Every opportunity I have been given to *shepherd the flock of God* I have done with a joyful, willing, and glad heart, knowing that Jesus entrusts me to feed, protect, and guide His people to freedom in Him. Just as the shepherds in the land of Israel would go before the sheep to lead them (not drive them), I too would go before God's people by providing meetings where many from most denominations would gather to worship the Lord in jubilant praise and dance. One such gathering happened in Southeast Alaska.

HEAVEN'S GLORY TOUCHES JUNEAU, ALASKA

I have always had a place in my heart for God's people and particularly for my Indian people, so when I watched the videotape of a missionary to Mexico's Indians named David, I invited him to come and bless our people. I knew he was a man of God who loved the Mexican Indians and trained them to flow with the Great Holy Spirit, seeing almost every body part re-created and the dead brought back to life. When I told him that my Indian people would come to hear him, he agreed to come for a July 2000 conference at a local venue.

When he arrived at the Juneau airport, I took a small band of Indians to welcome him to our city. After greeting him, I told him that all of us had been on a 40-day chain fast in preparation for the gathering, and he said, "I have too!" Trying to impress him, I told him that many believed for signs, wonders, and miracles to happen, and he grunted again, "I have too!" I thought, "A man of few words." Therefore, I left him alone, and we dropped him off at the hotel. On the first night of the meetings, after I had introduced Brother David, he went to the pulpit and did not greet us or tell us how beautiful our city was (which most visiting ministers do), but he opened the meeting by saying, "Y'all think you are so strong, but you have lost your pioneering spirit, and you are nothing but a bunch of wimps!" We all sat there in shocked disbelief.

Well, when the next night's meeting began, I went to the platform to welcome the audience and introduce David, and I said, "Brother David said last night that we have lost our Alaskan pioneering spirit, and we are nothing but a bunch of wimps! Well, all of you 'wimps' out there who think you are a 'mighty warrior,' I want you to stand up and give JESUS the biggest praise offering you can give Him!" The people jumped up, shouted, praised, whooped, and beat their tambourines and drums in honor to the King of kings and Lord of lords.

> The sound was almost deafening as it went into the heavenlies. Something broke that night, and Heaven's glory came down and touched Juneau. The power of God flowed through the aisles as two people walked out of their walkers, many were slain in the spirit, more were healed, and several were saved. When the healing power of Jesus healed a woman, she let go of her walker and began to walk on her own. As I was watching her walk, I heard the Spirit of the Lord say to me: "No longer will your people be bound; no longer will your people be restricted, but they will run with revival fire; they will run with My glory; they will run with Heaven's freedom; and

they will run with the good news of the new move of My Spirit." And run they did!

THE CROWN OF REJOICING

*Therefore we wanted to come to you—even I, Paul, time and again—but Satan hindered us. For what is our hope, or joy, or **crown of rejoicing**? Is it not even you in the presence of our Lord Jesus Christ at His coming? For you are our glory and joy (1 Thessalonians 2:18-20).*

MY VISION OF THE LION

Several years ago, I had a vision of the Christ witnessed by John, the revelator. In this vision, I was standing in front of two doors, and because of my insatiable curiosity, I reached out and turned the knob, wanting to see what might be lurking on the other side. What I saw when I opened the door left me shaking and gasping for breath. Before me sat the largest Lion I had ever seen. His eyes were deeply penetrating, and His huge form left my legs weak from fear and trembling. I did what you would have done in the face of fear—I slammed the door in His face! Somehow, I could see His form on the other side of the door. I watched as He tilted his head slightly to the right and then lifted that massive paw, putting it firmly on the door; and without any resistance, it swung open. Immediately I heard this Scripture in my spirit, "Behold, I stand at the door and knock..." (Rev. 3:21). Then I heard Jesus say, "Many evangelists use this Scripture to draw in the lost, but this Word is not for the lost but for the Church." He continued in His conversation with me and concluded, "Tell them Flo, I will no longer knock at the door of My own church, but tell them I am coming in whether they like it or not!"

There is coming to the Church in these last days a holy fear of the Lord, which the writer of Proverbs says, *"…is the beginning of wisdom…"* (Prov. 9:10). Many will come to a saving knowledge that their bodies are the *"…temple of the Holy Spirit…and you are not your own for you were bought at a price…"* (1 Cor. 6:19-20). This will bring great liberty to those who will embrace the confines of the Lord so that He might be glorified in their lives and ministries.

WHAT DO YOU WANT ME TO DO FOR YOU?

In Mark 10:32-45, the disciples are on their way to Jerusalem, and for the third time, Jesus predicts His death and resurrection. Jesus began to open up His deepest thoughts with those He had chosen, trusted, and loved. He had spent countless hours training and equipping them as the next revivalists. They had been with Him for three years; He was about to depart from the earth in great suffering and ultimately rise in victory. He shares His heart with them, saying, *"Behold, we are going up to Jerusalem, and the Son of Man will be betrayed to the chief priests and to the scribes. They will condemn Him to death and deliver Him to the Gentiles; and they will mock Him, scourge Him, spit on Him, and kill Him. And on the third day, He will rise again"* (Mark 10:33-34).

However, they did not hear a word He said to them! Have you ever been talking with someone in a meeting, and right in the middle of sharing your heart with them, they become preoccupied—looking past you, waving at a new-found "friend," and walking away from you? You are left feeling exposed and wounded in your emotions. That is what the disciples did to Jesus.

After Jesus told them in graphic detail of his torture and agony, James and John—the sons of thunder—came to Him and said, *"Teacher, we want You to do for us whatever we ask"* (Mark 10:35).

In the past two millennia, humanity has not changed much. May I be very candid with you? Many of us in this current move of God called the "river of God" are still in this for ourselves. The purpose of the River of God that flows from the Throne of God in Revelation 22:1 is first of all purification, and it sweeps over us to effect a permanent change in us, but we have been frolicking in the river until we have become like unruly children. What we sometimes call the "river glory" is nothing more than revelry or noisy partying, and it is all about us.

Like James and John (in our continuing story), we too might be saying, *"Teacher, we want You to do for us whatever we ask!"* In Mark 10:36, Jesus said to the brothers (I can hear a slight agitation in His voice), *"What do you want Me to do for you?"* They responded to Him in a childish, charismatic way, *"Grant us that we may sit, one on Your right hand and the other on Your left, in your glory"* (Mark 10:37). To ask to share His throne with Him was a little presumptuous, since they were still vying for position and prestige. Eight times in the Book of Revelation, Jesus speaks of the promises available *"to him that overcomes…"* And in Revelation 3:21, He says, *"To him who overcomes I will grant to sit with Me on My throne…."*

You have to first be overcome before you can overcome.

The Cup and the Baptism

Jesus went on to ask James and John a provocative question, *"You do not know what you ask. Are you able to drink the cup that I drink; and be baptized with the baptism that I am baptized with?"* *"We are able!"* They said charismatically! *"We are able!"* (Mark 10:38-39). Sometimes we do not have a clue what we are saying.

We speak prematurely, without fully thinking it through. After they spoke with careless ease, Jesus said to them, *"You will indeed drink the cup that I drink, and with the baptism I am baptized with you will be baptized; but to sit on My right hand and on My left is not Mine to give, but it is for those for whom it is prepared"* (Mark 10:39-40).

The cup they would drink was the cup of suffering. Philippians 1:29 says, *"For to you it is given on behalf of Christ, not only to believe in Him, but also to suffer for His sake."* The cup of suffering was also the cup of blessing. In First Corinthians 11:25-26, Paul recounts Jesus' words during the last supper: *"This cup is the new testament in My blood: this do ye, as oft as ye drink it, in remembrance of Me. For as often as ye eat this bread and drink this cup, ye do shew the Lord's death till He comes"* (KJV).

Jesus requires more than taking of the emblems for our health and well-being. He requires the giving of our lives too, for just as He shed His blood for humanity, He wants us to give our lives for the world. We all know and can quote John 3:16: *"For God so loved the world that He gave His only begotten Son, that whoever believes in Him should not perish, but have everlasting life."* However, most of us cannot quote First John 3:16 which says, *"By this we know love, because He laid down His life for us. And we also ought to lay down our lives for the brethren."*

After drinking the cup, the promise is *"and with the baptism I am baptized with you will be baptized."* The disciples did not understand the depth of the cost of their commitment, but Jesus did. To carry them through the severe trials that they would soon encounter, Jesus promised to send them the powerful Holy Spirit Who was called the Comforter, the Paraclete, or Helper who would come alongside them. This Helper would eventually live inside of them to instruct, guide, teach, and empower them to live a life of victory to the end. Jesus promised them that He would baptize them with the Holy Spirit and fire. This baptism would keep them humble. He finished by saying, *"And whoever of you desires to be first shall be slave of all. For even the son of Man did not come to be served, but to serve, and to give His life a ransom for many"* (Mark 10:44-45).

After the discussion of who was the greatest and who would sit on the throne with Jesus, they came to Jericho, where a great crowd was following them. When a blind man named Bartimaeus heard it was Jesus, he starting crying out in a loud voice, *"Jesus, Son of David, have mercy on me!"* (Mark 10:47). Nevertheless, because of the noise, Jesus did not hear him. The crowd continued to walk on.

Bartimaeus was not going to let this opportunity pass him by.

He had been in that condition long enough, and that day was his day for his healing. He cried out again; many tried to shut him up and could not because of his desperation: *"Son of David,* [he knew that, if He was truly the Messiah, then He was God and had all power] *have mercy on me!"* Moreover, the Bible makes an amazing statement, *"so Jesus stood still...."* Imagine that, at the cry of one person, the God of Heaven and earth stood still! Think about that! *"...and He commanded him to be called"* (Mark 10:49). Bartimaeus stood upon his feet, threw off his filthy garment, and went to stand in front of the King of kings. Jesus asked him with tender compassion, *"What do you want Me to do for you?"* (Mark 10:51). There is that same question again! Bartimaeus may have thought, can't you see I am blind?

Nevertheless, Jesus wanted him to articulate his need. The blind man said to Him, *"Rabboni,* [which is a tender word in Aramaic meaning 'master'] *I want to receive my sight"* (Mark 10:51). *I am tired of sitting in the dirt; I want to walk like a man. Jesus must have thought, He is the reason I came to give my life, so that he might live and be made well.* With tender mercy, Jesus tells him to go his way—his faith had made him well: *"And immediately he received his sight and followed Jesus on the road"* (Mark 10:52).

Jesus asked the same question of both James and John, the "sons of thunder," and of Bartimaeus. *"What do you want Me to do for you?"* The sons of thunder were blinded by their own pride, and Bartimaeus was blinded by a physical condition—all three were blinded by the devil, and all three were *healed* by Jesus—oh, the mercy of our God!

FOOT WASHING IN MEXICO

When the '85 Mexico crusade was over, the 35 pastors (the same 35 pastors who did not know that I had never preached before that crusade) were so overjoyed at the salvations, healings, and miracles that they wanted to have a picnic in my honor. I did not like that idea, but they were insistent. They had no money to give me as an honorarium, so they killed the "fatted calf," and we had barbecued beef and wonderful side dishes of fresh tomatoes, hot peppers, cilantro, onions, and avocados. I was sitting at the head table with my interpreter's wife, and we were enjoying the delicious food and light conversation. I had just put a fork full of beef into my mouth and was relishing the flavor when I saw from the corner of my eye a man accompanying a woman, who was carrying a large tray of freshly-barbecued beef, heading in my direction.

I turned to look at them, and before I could greet them, the elder said to me, "This woman has a *great* desire to wash your feet." Instantly my eyes filled with tears, and I cried silently to the Lord, "Lord, am I so proud of what happened here in Mexico that You need to humble me?" He did not answer me. I reached for my napkin to put the freshly-chewed beef into it when he cried out, "No, she wants you to finish eating." I said to him, "How can I finish eating now?" As gracefully as I could, I pulled one leg, and then another out from under the long pew and walked meekly away from the table, following her like a sheep to the slaughter. She walked quietly before me, and we went into a shanty.

When I stepped in, I sensed the pristine presence of a holy God. The room was sparsely furnished with a loveseat up against the wall and a lone chair in the middle of the room; a basin full of water was sitting on the floor in front of the chair. There were two young women sitting on the loveseat to witness what was about to happen. The woman motioned for me to sit down and to take off my pantyhose, but I shook my head no, so she proceeded. She gingerly picked up one foot and put it in the cool water. She cupped her hand with water and let it trickle down my ankle onto my toes. She lovingly picked up the next foot and did the same. As I sat there, my emotions were everywhere.

I was sobbing and asking the Lord, "Have I stepped into pride? Have I disappointed You? Have I touched Your glory? Have I...have I...have I?" He never answered one question. When she finished, I motioned to her (she could not speak English, and I could not understand Spanish) to sit on the chair so I could in turn wash her feet, and she shook her head almost violently with an emphatic, "NO!" Choked with tears, I left that "sanctuary" feeling languid and unworthy, and I flew back to Juneau, Alaska.

A couple weeks later, early in the morning, I was reading from John 13:1-17:

> *Now before the Feast of the Passover, when Jesus knew that His hour had come that He should depart from this world to the Father, having loved His own who were in the world, He loved them to the end. And supper being ended...[He] rose from supper and laid aside His garments, took a towel and girded Himself. After that, He poured water into a basin and began to wash the disciples' feet....*

The Living Bible says, "O how He loved them...He tied a towel around Himself and began to wash their feet..." As I was reading from the Living Bible, the revelation of what happened in that shanty in Mexico slowly began to roll up in me, and then I heard Jesus say to me, "Flo, that was not a woman who washed your feet. I washed your feet! I have called many to take my Gospel to the nations, but they refused...but you went, and because you went, I wanted to honor you and wash your feet. Flo, I love you, and I appreciate what you did for Me in My name. For now, I simply say 'Thank you,' but in the life to come, you will receive a great reward." When He finished speaking to me, I wept loudly as I raised my hands in worship to the only One who is worthy of such adoration—Jesus Christ, my Lord and Savior. I do not know how long I cried and worshipped, my heart bursting with love for Him. As I sat there, I resolved that whatever He wanted of me I would gladly do—even to the giving of my life that others might live.

In Second Timothy 4:1-8, Paul gives Timothy this mandate:

*I charge you therefore before God and the Lord Jesus Christ, who will judge the living and the dead at His appearing and His kingdom: Preach the word! Be ready in season and out of season. Convince, rebuke, exhort, with all longsuffering and teaching. For the time will come when they will not endure sound doctrine, but according to their own desires, because they have itching ears, they will heap up for themselves teachers; and they will turn their ears away from the truth, and be turned aside to fables. But you be watchful in all things, endure afflictions, do the work of an evangelist, fulfill your ministry. For I am already being poured out as a drink offering, and the time of my departure is at hand. I have fought a good fight, I have finished my race, I have kept the faith. Finally there is laid up for me the **crown of righteousness,** which the Lord, the righteous Judge, will give to me on that Day, and not to me only but to all who have loved His appearing* (2 Timothy 4:1-8).

Only those who are living a holy life, who are dead to themselves and alive to Him, will be waiting for His second coming. And when Jesus comes for you, He will give you *the imperishable crown* for your steadfastness; *the crown of life* for all your soul winning efforts; *the crown of glory* for your endurance to the end; *the crown of rejoicing* for your labor of love on your earth's journey; and *the crown of righteousness* for your preparedness at His second coming. Are *you* prepared?

ENDNOTE

1. Charles G. Finney, *How to Experience Revival* (New Kensington, PA: Whitaker House, 1986), 7.

Additional copies of this book and other book titles from DESTINY IMAGE are available at your local bookstore.

Call toll-free: 1-800-722-6774

Send a request for a catalog to:

Destiny Image® Publishers, Inc.
P.O. Box 310
Shippensburg, PA 17257-0310

"Speaking to the Purposes of God for This Generation and for the Generations to Come."

For a complete list of our titles, visit us at www.destinyimage.com

ACTIVATING
THE ANGELIC